The Power of Recognizing Intent: From Social Skills to AI Safety

Quinn

Table of Contents

Chapter 1: Introduction

April, 1944, in the midst of WWII, Gestalt psychologists Fritz Heider and Marianne Simmel published a seminal work *"An Experimental Study of Apparent Behavior"* [42] with only one animation studied (Figure 1.1)

Figure 1.1: [Video] Animation used in (Heider and Simmel, 1944). Please click the image to play the video (Adobe Acrobat Reader required). Full animation can be viewed at `https://youtu.be/VTNmLt7QX8E`.

When we look at this animation (Figure 1.1), we see not only moving triangles and circles, but also a vivid story of one bullies two. The two being bullied, one brave and another timid, work together to trick the big bully and escape, leaving the bully in anger and frustration. How come we can so easily see those geometric objects as living beings, having emotions, intention or even personality? Answering this question, however, is not an easy feat. The ability to think about mental states of others is coined "Theory of Mind" (ToM) by [76] as it forms a "theory" of others' minds. This cognitive function provides a vast range of inference tools for human, including inference on others' belief, desire, knowledge, emotion, intention, etc.

Among many capabilities of human ToM, recognizing the intentionality of an action (intentional or not) is considered an important aspect [89]. Not only does it enable a further high-level action analysis when necessary, it is also a pivot in moral judgement. With this significance, people might found it surprising that the current understanding on the neural underpinning of visual perception of intentionality in human brain, as well as intentionality recognition in machine intelligence, is largely unexplored.

This dissertation is a series of attempts to understand how humans recognize intentionality from visual input and how can we leverage this knowledge to equip machine with such computational capability.

In the rest of this introduction, a brief background on the prior arts will be described to establish the significance of the problem and its difficulty (detailed existed literature will be described in each Chapter independently). Chapter arrangement of this dissertation will be described in Section 1.3.

1.1 Significance on Understanding Intentionality Recognition

When talking about understanding a cognitive function (or a complex computational system in general), what does it exactly mean by "understanding"? To answer this, we can borrow the three-level framework proposed by David Marr, which is understanding on Computational level, Algorithmic level and Implementational level [60]:

- Computational level: What is the goal of computation? Why are they appropriate? What is the overall logic and strategy for the computation?

- Representation and Algorithmic level: To achieve this computation, what representation is appropriate for the input/output? What is the algorthmic procedure for this specific computation?

- Implementational level: What physical implementation can be used for the representation and algorithms?

An example commonly used is a calculator. At computational level, it needs to carry out arithmetic operations. At representation and algorithmic level, Arabic numberals can be used for the representations, and the rules of about adding from the lowest digit to the highest and "carry" to the next digit if the sum exceeds 9 can be used as the algorithm. At implementation level, we can use binary-coded decimal and logic gate or using 10-notch gear and specially designed gear train.

Having equipped with the knowledge on what is "understanding". It is possible then to discuss the significance of the intentionality recognition, which lies in three-fold, for basic science, for medical advancement, for high-level automation.

Understanding human visual recognition of intentionality is a part of understanding human brain. As main organ for human intelligence, understanding human brain is part of the most important basic research [107, 14]. World's major players in science community have all launched their neuroscience initiatives with United States' BRAIN initiative [90], European Union's Human Brain Project (HBP) [6], Chinese China Brain Project (CBP) [75], Japanese Brain/MINDS project [70], etc.

But more practically, understanding intention recognition provides possibility to address the factors that affects human's capability of recognizing intent. Studies reported that subgroups with Autism disorder might found difficulties recognizing non-intentional actions and accidental harm [74, 68], criticizing others' accidental mistakes more harshly than their neurotypical counterparts. Patients with major depression and alcoholism also shows decreasing capability of ToM including intent inferences [101, 102]. Intention and intentionality recognition is also crucial for the effectiveness and safety of powered prosthesis with neural control and feedback [69, 59] which can potentially drastically improve the life quality of disabled individuals.

On the aspect of high-level automation and machine intelligence, the significance on recognizing intention can be shown through a simple example in autonomous driving. When a human driver sees a pedestrian moving, the intent of the pedestrian will be inferred by the driver to determine the next sequence of actions. If the pedestrian approaches the boundary of the side walk and looks left and right, the driver might infer that this pedestrian plan to cross the street. Upon recognizing this intent, the driver might start to slow and stop the car, letting the pedestrian cross. For an autonomous driving agent, without the capability of recognizing intent, the car might not yield to the pedestrian, potentially violating traffic regulation or even causing an accident.

1.2 Difficulties of Intentionality Recognition

In this dissertation, we primarily focuses on recognizing the intentionality of an action, i.e., if an action is intentional or not. The word intentionality and intentional used here should not be confused with the Intentionality and Intentional (with a captial I) in philosophy literatures, where the Intentionality refers to the property of mental states (or event) by which they are directed (at some other external matters) [89]. Under a philosophical context, a belief is Intentional since if I have a belief then I must believe in something. Fear is also Intentional since it associates with fear of something or some events.

The intentionality and intentional concept used in this dissertation are commonsense based, which is similar to how typical emotion categories (like happy, sad, etc.) or objects categories (like cars, chairs, etc.) are defined in research literature. This commonsense perception of intentionality is better shown with examples. When we observe the actions in Figure 1.2, the human movements on the left is clearly intentional while the movement on the right is clearly non-intentional. This recognition is automatic, effortless and shared among people.

(a) Example of intentional action.

(b) Example of non-intentional action.

Figure 1.2: [Video] Examples of intentional and non-intentional actions. The perception of intentional and non-intentional action are generally shared across people. Actions in video (a) can be easily perceived as intentional and (b) non-intentional. Please click the image to play the video (Adobe Acrobat Reader required).

Having a commonsense definition of intentionality does not imply triviality of the problem. Quite the opposite, it indicates the concept itself is highly complex (thus there is lack of better way to rigorously define the concept). Studies in psychology has shown that the perception on intentionality of an action is related to belief, desire, awareness of the action and skill of the agent [58]. The commonsense concept becomes more complicate in the context of strong moral bias as [51] shows that moral judgement can actually affect the perception of intentionality. These studies, although shows potential hypothetical mechanism for intentionality recognition, are based on language based vignettes (short stories) rather than visual input (our interest). The tool of language is able to provide description on the agent's mental state and skill level which are not readily available from mere visual stimuli. Thus, the visual recognition of intentionality is arguably even more complicated (and thus fascinating) than the language based recognition.

1.3 Chapter Arrangement

Having established the significance and difficulty on understanding intentionality recognition, the rest of this dissertation will describe four studies aim to address this issue.

On the implementational level, Chapter 2 presents an functional magnetic resonance imaging (fMRI) study to investigate which areas of human brain hosts the computation of visual recognition of intent. On the computational and algorithmic level, Chapter 3 presents a study to construct a machine learning algorithm that able to generate intentional and non-intentional actions performed by an abstract geometric agent and the corresponding environmental context. Chapter 4 presents a machine learning algorithm that can generate intentional and non-intentional actions performed by human agent and imagine counterfactual actions. Chapter 5 is a study I cooperated with Stuart Synakowsky, which proposes a common-sense based intentionality recognition instead of a data-driven learning algorithm, which can be applied on both abstract spherical agent and realistic human agents.

Chapter 6 concludes the dissertation with a discussion on the current results and their implication to future directions.

Chapter 2: Brain Mechanisms of the Visual Recognition of Intent in Humans

While many individual aspects of visual perception, social interactions, and theory of mind have been investigated before [45, 50, 82, 36, 35, 83, 86], the exact neural and computational mechanisms for the visual analysis of intent have not been systematically studied. This is surprising, since many philosophers and scientists have emphasized the relevance of intent recognition and its role in the development of societies and government. Aristotle, in his book Rhetoric [8], was one of the first philosophers to formally define intent as something deliberate that was chosen before the performed behavior. These views were transformed by Descartes [27] when he introduced Cartesian dualism in which conscious intent is differentiated from behavioral reflexes caused by external stimuli. Later, Darwin [24] beautifully articulated the importance of intent recognition for the evolution of cooperative behavior and argued that this has allowed humans to successfully build large, advanced societies.

Here, we study the neural mechanisms involved in this complex ability, i.e., the visual recognition of intent. We hypothesize that to perform this very difficult inference, our cognitive system must draw from a number of brain regions. Specifically, we hypothesize that regions involved in the analysis of biological motion, theory of mind, and bodies are recruited to interpret intent in others. Biological motion is expected to play a major role in this visual recognition, since it is this ability that allows people to assess the behaviors of others [91, 88, 87]. Similarly, theory of mind areas should help interpret the behavior of others and are thus expected to contribute to the visual recognition of others' intent [86]. Other brain mechanisms, as those involved in place and object recognition may sometimes contribute too, but only when these attributes are necessary to interpret the scene or contextualize a behavior. However, herein, we are primarily interested in the essential mechanisms of the visual recognition of intent, even in minimalist, abstract videos with little or no information on specific objects and scenes.

To this end, we present two experiments where participants watched a set of videos of 3D geometric objects moving with and without intent while in the MRI (Magnetic Resonance Imaging). Using MVPA (multivariate pattern analysis) on BOLD (blood-oxygen-level dependent) fMRI (functional MRI) data, we show that the above-listed brain areas are indeed involved in the decoding of intentional versus non-intentional behaviors. We also show that ROIs devoted to other visual tasks, such as motion detection, character and face recognition as well as early visual areas do not contribute to this visual recognition.

2.1 Result

2.1.1 Stimuli

Consider the following two visual scenarios. There is a slanted surface (i.e., a ramp) with a few round boxes on the floor. First, a small ball appears and we see it rolling down. When the ball collides with a box, it rolls about it and continues its downward motion. On seeing this, we do not attribute intentionality to the ball since its motion obviously is purely driven by gravity. A bit later, a person appears and starts walking down the same

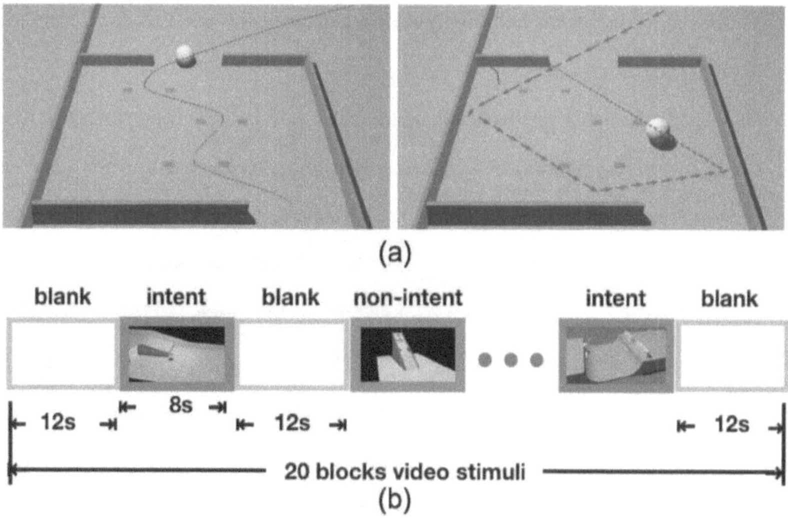

Figure 2.1: a. Participants watched videos with stationary and moving objects. Some of these corresponded to intentional behaviors (left), whereas other do not (right). In these images, arrows indicate the trajectory followed by each the ball and the size of the arrow its velocity. b. The fMRI Experiment 1 uses a block design. In each run participants watched 20 videos; one video per block. Each video lasted 8 seconds and was preceded by a 12 second blank screen. The experiment included 6 runs. There was a 12 second blank screen at the end of each run to allocate for data shifting in the analysis.

slanted surface, avoiding the boxes as she walks down. Here, we say that the person had the intention of walking down and avoiding the obstacles.

We might be tempted to think that by understanding that a person has intent while a ball does not, the problem of recognizing intent is solved. As eloquently illustrated by Heider and Simmel [43] (see Figure 1.1), this could not be further from the truth. In their classical experiment, we see a set of two-dimensional geometric figures moving on a plane;

despite its visual simplicity, we quickly and effortlessly start attributing intent to each of the objects' movements.

Following this approach, we generated 80 videos of 3D balls moving in minimalist, geometric environments, Figure 2.1(a). Half of these videos show behaviors of an intentional nature. The other half correspond to non-intentional behaviors. The videos were then uploaded to Amazon Mechanical Turk. 30 subjects watched the videos and indicated whether the perceived behavior was intentional or not. Tables in Appendix A show the percentage of times subjects selected intent and non-intent for each of the 80 videos. These percentages indicate the easiness of interpreting intent in each video. We selected the easiest 60 videos (i.e., those with agreement > 90%) for Experiment 1, and the 20 most difficult, non-obvious videos (with an agreement between 55 and 83%) for Experiment 2. For more details about the method are described in Section 2.3.1. Figure 2.2 shows a pair of intentional and non-intentional videos used in experiment 1.

(a) Example of intentional action.   (b) Example of non-intentional action.

Figure 2.2: [Video] Examples of intentional and non-intentional stimuli used in the experiments. (a) shows two guards walk down stairs and capture someone in the cell. (b) shows the corresponding non-intentional physical movement of three balls in the exact same scene. Please click the image to play the video (Adobe Acrobat Reader required).

2.1.2 Experiment 1

Participants watched the 60 videos described above; one at a time. Participants did not perform any task and were only instructed to watch the videos attentively. Videos lasted 8 seconds and were separated by a 12 second blank screen, Figure 2.1b. The order of the videos was randomized, such that each participant watched them in a different order (more details see Section 2.3.3: Experiment 1). The entire process was repeated twice. We also used localizers to identify the ROIs (regions of interest) for Theory of Mind (ToM), motion detection (MT+), as well as those associated with face, character, body and place recognition (Section 2.3.3: Localizers). Ten subjects completed the experiment.

We performed across- and between-subject analyses using MVPA on the BOLD signal. In both cases, the BOLD data is first pre-processed and mapped to MNI (more details see Section 2.3.4). Thus, for each ROI, the elements of each feature vector define the voxels in MNI, $\mathbf{x}_{ij} = (x_{ij1}, \ldots, x_{ijp})^T$, with p the number of voxels in MNI, and x_{ijk} the BOLD signal of the kth voxel of the jth acquisition of the ith subject. Recall that each video of an intentional or non-intentional behavior lasts 8 seconds, which (with a TR=2s) corresponds to 4 acquisitions per video. We computed the average of these four acquisitions, $\bar{\mathbf{x}}_{il} = (\bar{x}_{il1}, \ldots, \bar{x}_{ilp})^T$, where l specifies the video number (i.e., $l = 1, \ldots, 120$, since each video is watched twice), and $\bar{x}_{ilj} = 0.25 \sum_{j \in \text{video}l} x_{ilj}$. Then, we use PCA (Principal Component Analysis) [61] to reduce the dimensionality of this p-dimensional feature representation to q dimensions, i.e., $\hat{\mathbf{x}}_{il} = (\hat{x}_{il1}, \ldots, \hat{x}_{ilq})^T$. The value of q is set to guarantee that about 90% of the variance of the data is preserved in the lower q-dimensional space [71].

Classification accuracy of intentional versus non-international behaviors is computed in this q-dimensional PCA space using Linear Discriminant Analysis (LDA) [40]. The results

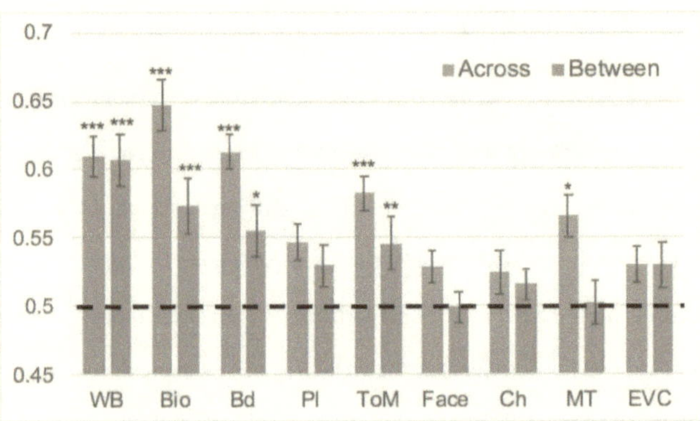

Figure 2.3: Results of Experiment 1. Shown here are the results of the across- and between-subject analyses (blue and orange bars, respectively). Error bars indicate standard error (SE). Statistical significance is computed using a permutation test (Section 2.3.4: Statistical Significance). * p<.01, ** p<.001, *** p<.0001. WB: Whole Brain; Bio: Biological motion area in pSTS; Bd: Body area; Pl: place areas; ToM: Theory of Mind areas; Face: face areas; Ch: character recognition area; MT: motion area; EVC: early visual cortex.

are in Figure 2.3, with the blue bars specifying the classification accuracy of the across-subject analysis and the orange bars the between-subject analysis. The across-subjects results are given by a leave-one-pair out cross-validation analysis, where all subjects' data are concatenated together. This means that, at each iteration, a video of an intentional and a video of a non-intentional behavior (for all subjects) are not used to train the LDA classifier and are instead used to test it. This process is repeated for each pair of intentional-non-intentional videos in Table S1. To compute the between-subject results we used a leave-one-subject out cross-validation approach. This means that the data of all subjects but one are used to train the LDA classifier, while the data of the left-out subject are used to compute the classification accuracy. This is repeated for each subject we can leave out. Figure 2.3 shows the average classification accuracies of these tests and the standard error. Statistical significance is computed using a permutation test (Section 2.3.4 Statistical significance).

Figure 2.3 shows the results of the LDA decoder when using all the voxels in the brain (i.e., a whole brain analysis) as well as the voxels in single ROIs. Specifically, we show the results when using the voxels in the ROI of biological motion, bodies, places, ToM, faces, characters, MT+, and early visual cortex (EVC).

These results show that we can reliably decode the perception of intentional vs. non-intentional behaviors in the whole brain analysis ($p<.0001$) and in the ROI responsible for the perception of biological motion ($p<.0001$). ToM and bodies ROIs are also important contributors to the visual analysis of intent, but less so than the biological motion area ($p<.001$ and $p<.01$,respectively). Additionally, and as expected, areas dedicated to the perception of faces, characters and motion as well as EVC do not show significant visual decoding of intent (all p's$>.05$). These results are in support of our hypothesis.

Another way to pinpoint the regions that most contribute to the visual analysis of intent is by identifying the most discriminant voxels provided by our classifier in the whole brain analysis. This is given by the highest discriminant scores of LDA [94]. To see this, recall that LDA assigns a discriminant score to each voxel (Section 2.3.4 Reprojection maps). These discriminant scores can be plotted in MNI to identify the most discriminant ROIs. Specifically, we identified the voxels that contribute most to the decoding of intent. The results are in Figure 2.4. As we can appreciate in the figure, the most discriminant voxels span the most posterior part of the right STS, reaching up to the temporoparietal junction (TPJ). These brain regions are associate with the perception of biological motion and theory or mind, respectively [91, 116], further supporting our hypothesis.

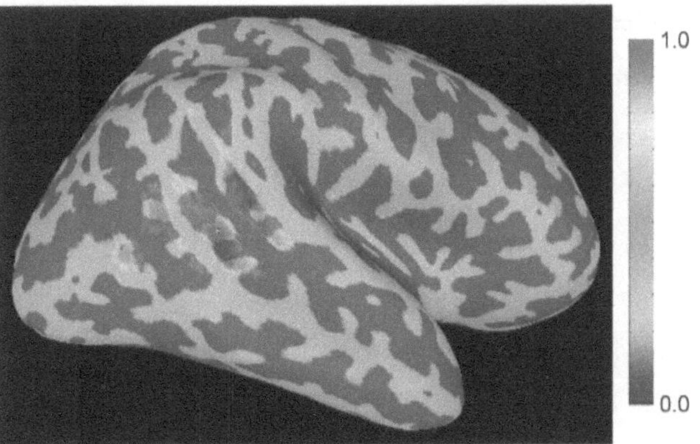

Figure 2.4: Shown here are the most important voxels in the visual decoding of intent, as per our MVPA analysis. The relevance values of each voxel have been normalized. The scale is given by the colormap shown on right, with 1.0 specifying the most discriminant voxels.

2.1.3 Experiment 2

To further assess our hypothesis, we study the neural decoding ability in these areas as the intentionality of the observed behavior becomes ambiguous, i.e., cases where people are much less accurate in the interpretation of intent. To test this, we selected the 20 videos that our subjects in the Amazon Mechanical Turk experiment found easy and the 20 videos they found difficult to classify as intentional or non-intentional. If our hypothesized ROIs are indeed responsible for the visual recognition of intent, then decoding should be highly accurate in the 20 easy videos and close to chance in the difficult videos. That is, if these ROIs are indeed the brain areas used to visually interpret intent, then decoding of intent in these ROIs should be proportional to people's behavioral response. Specifically, we selected the first 20 videos in Table S1, which are readily interpreted by humans, and the bottom 20 videos in this table, which people find difficult or impossible to interpret.

This experiment followed the same procedure outlined in Experiment 1: Participants watched 8 second videos, separated by 12 second blanks, Figure 2.1b. Participants were asked to pay attention to what was happening in the video, but there was no task. The order of the videos was randomized across participants. Thus, each participant watched the videos in a different order. The participants were the same as in Experiment 1 (Section 2.3.3: Experiment 2).

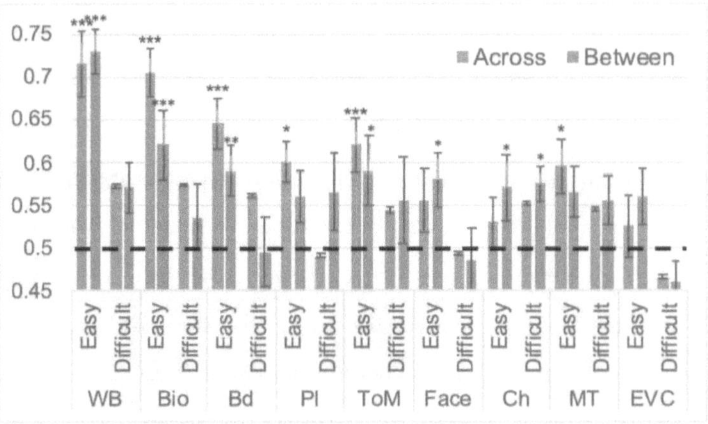

Figure 2.5: a. Results of Experiment 2. Here, we computed the MVPA decoding of intent in easy and difficult videos. We note that this decoding is consistent with the behavior marker of difficulty in interpreting intent in the observed behavior. Bars specify the average classification accuracy; error bars denote standard error. Blue bars show the results of the across-subject analysis, which is given by a leave-one-video-pair out cross validation test. The between-subject results, computed using a leave-one-subject out test, are in orange. Statistical significance is given by a permutation test. * p<.01, ** p<.001, *** p<.0001.

Next, we trained the PCA+LDA classifier described above using a subset of data of Experiment 1 and test it using the data of Experiment 2. Care was taken not to use the same videos in training and testing. To do this, when an easy video is used for testing, it is removed from the training set. This process is repeated 20 times, for each of the videos that can be left out. Average classification accuracies and standard errors of this approach are given in Figure 2.5. In this figure, blue bars specify the decoding when doing an across-subject analysis; orange bars correspond to a between-subject analysis (Section 2.3.4: Across-subject analysis and Between-subject analysis). We provide results of a whole brain analysis as well as those of each ROI. Each of these results are separated into the decoding attained when testing on the videos that are easily interpreted by humans and those that are found difficult or nearly impossible.

As expected, we found the biological motion, ToM and body ROIs to contribute most to the visual recognition of intent. Crucially, these results only hold when the behavior in the videos are readily interpretable as intentional or non-intentional. When the videos show difficult-to-interpret behaviors, we are unable to decode intent from these brain regions. These results support the hypothesis that the brain mechanisms dedicated to biological motion, ToM and visual analysis of bodies are involved in the visual recognition of intent. Furthermore, when the videos are visually non-interpretable by participants, these brain areas are unable to successfully interpret the visual cues in these videos.

To further study this last point, we pinpointed the most discriminant ROI used when participants watched the difficult-to-interpret videos by identifying the most discriminant voxels in the whole brain analysis, Figure 2.6(a-b). As can be appreciated in the figure, in contrast to Experiment 1, none of the hypothesized brain regions are most discriminant of intent when the behavior cannot be robustly visually interpreted. Indeed, it is important

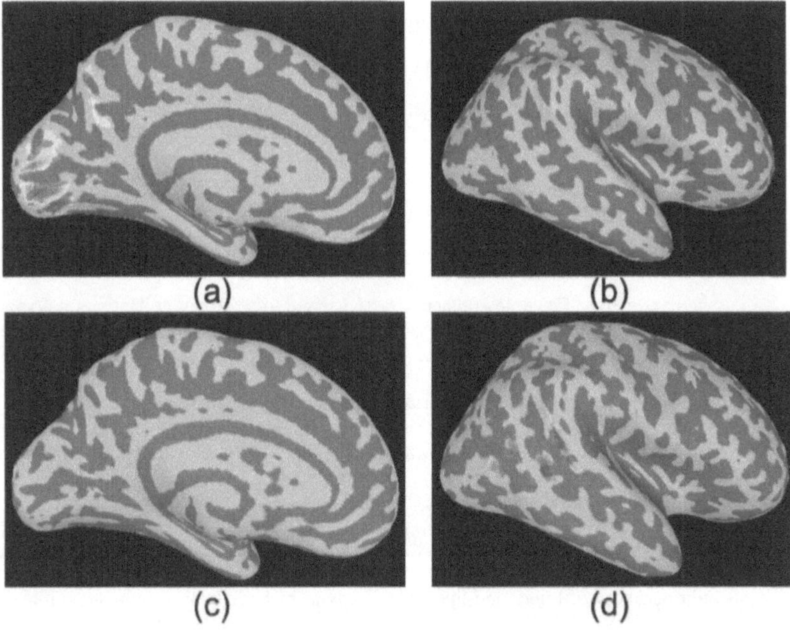

Figure 2.6: a-b. Shown here are the most relevant voxels of the visual decoding of intent when watching the difficult to interpret videos. The cluster shown here is bilateral. c-d. The most discriminant voxels of the visual decoding of intent when watching the easy to interpret videos. The relevance of voxels has been normalized to values between 0 and 1 (see colormap in Figure 2.4). Medial view, left side (b and d). Lateral view, right side (c and e). We see that the hypothesized areas can only decode intent when that readily visually recognized by human observers.

to note that while the brain region shown in Figure 2.6(c-d) corresponds to the voxels with highest discriminant scores, even this region does not provide statistically significant discriminability of intent for these difficult videos (p>.6), supporting the behavioral results of Table S1. Nonetheless, the region shown in Figure 2.6(a-b) corresponds to the voxels with highest discriminant scores. In contrast, when we repeat this approach on the data of the videos humans find easy to interpret as intentional or not, the hypothesized areas are the most discriminant, Figure 2.6(c-d).

2.2   Discussion

Intent plays an important role in our lives. For example, the courts typically apply much stricter penalties if an unlawful action was deemed to be committed intentionally compared to those done non-intentionally [11, 5, 116]. People also report increased suffering when an action is perceived to be performed intentionally, compared to when the same harm is done non-intentionally [38]. But, what are the neural mechanisms that allow us to interpret whether an observed behavior is intentional or not?

Our hypothesis was that the ROIs dedicated to the analysis of an agent's biological motion, theory of mind, and the visual analysis of bodies allow humans to make this determination. Using a set of minimalistic, geometric scenes and agents (as in the classical Heider and Simmel (1944) work, Figure 2.1) and MVPA on BOLD fMRI data, we showed strong evidence in favor of this hypothesis. Specifically, in our first experiment, we were able to decode whether an observed video showed an intentional or a non-intentional behavior using multivariate decoding on these ROIs. We demonstrated efficient decoding ability in both across- and between-subject analyses.

Importantly, our results support the hypothesis that the visual recognition of intent is primarily associated with the brain areas dedicated to the interpretation of biological motion, theory of mind, and bodies. Our hypothesis was supported both by the ROI analysis in Figure 2.3 and the whole-brain analysis highlighting the most discriminant voxels in

Figure 2.4. Importantly, low-level visual areas such as early visual cortex and motion-selective MT+ could not decode this information, confirming that our results were not simply a byproduct of low-level visual differences between the videos, but rather reflect the visual recognition of intent.

We know, however, that our ability to infer intentionality from behavior is not always accurate [17]. In some cases, an action is deemed intentional even when it is not, yielding stricter sentences in court. We thus hypothesized that we should not find significant decoding of intentionality in the brain regions associated with the processing of biological motion, theory of mind and bodies when participants watch difficult-to-interpret intentional behaviors.

To test this, in our second experiment, we showed participants videos with behaviors that are either easy or difficult to interpret as intentional by humans. We found that while our decoding of intentionality from the hypothesized ROIs was excellent for the easy videos, it was about chance for the difficult ones. This result provides the strongest evidence yet that the hypothesized brain areas are indeed associated with the visual recognition of intent: When subjects can readily interpret intentionality, these brain areas are shown to decode it. But when subjects have a hard time interpreting the intentionality of an action, the neural pattern of activity in these areas is similarly ambiguous.

Of the brain areas confirmed by our experiments as being involved in the visual recognition of intent, the ROI associated with the perception of biological motion stands out. This is not surprising. Similar regions in pSTS have been found to interpret social interactions amongst several agents, and even determining if these interactions have positive or negative valence [45, 78, 108, 35]; similar brain areas have been identified in other primates as well [92]. Also, nearby voxels have been found to decode facial actions from human faces [94] and faces in other primates [100], a process that is essential to interpret social interactions, emotions and intentions from others.

Other brain areas believed to be responsible for the interpretation of people's behavior and emotion are the ROIs of ToM [96, 50, 52]. We find that, indeed, these brain areas play an important role in the visual interpretation of intent.

These results are not only essential to understand how humans recognize intent, but provide important knowledge for the design of machine learning and computer vision systems that wish to emulate this ability [3, 54]. Further, our results show that the neural decoding of intent in these regions closely tracks behavior, providing insight on how people correctly or incorrectly assign intent to observed behaviors, which could have implications for how our laws are interpreted and applied as well as in the assessment of moral and immoral behaviors.

2.3 Methods

The experimental design and protocol were approved by the Office of Responsible Research Practices at The Ohio State University (OSU).

2.3.1 Stimuli

The stimuli were synthesized 3D animation videos created using Autodesk's software Maya. All the videos are 8 seconds long, 60 frames per second, 1028x578 pixels per frame. Images are in b/w. Videos are designed in pairs. Each pair includes a video of an intentional behavior and one of a non-intentional behavior. These two behaviors show the same scene and the agents have somewhat similar dynamics, with one being intentional and the other one not intentional. The scene is given by simple geometric objects, and the agents by 3D balls, Figure 2.1(a). In each video, one or more agents move in a 3D scene containing a variety of stationary and/or moving objects. The light source, camera position, number of balls and scene are the same in each video pair. The only difference being the agents' behaviors. In the intentional video, the agents move with intent. Here, the balls movements are not only self-generated (without any external force responsible for the behavior), but also consistent with their perceived intention.

In contrast, in the non-intentional videos, the balls move merely according to the Newtonian laws of physics. To simulate Newtonian laws in our videos, gravity is set to $9.8 \, \mathrm{m/s^2}$, and the coefficient of restitution and friction simulate wooden or steel materials. These physical movements are simulated using the Bullet physical engine in Maya. We generate 80 video pairs, for a total of 160 videos. Thus, 80 videos show intentional behaviors, and 80 videos non-intentional behaviors.

2.3.2 Behavioral experiment

To assess the easiness of perception of intentional vs. non-intentional behaviors, we performed an online experiment on Amazon Mechanical Turk. Each subject watched each video (maximum twice per video) before specifying whether the observed behavior appears intentional or not. Every video was evaluated by 30 subjects. Percentage of agreement on the perception of intent or non-intent was computed. Table S1 lists the videos in order of percentage of agreement. Hence, the videos on top of the table correspond to those that are clearly and easily classifiable as intentional vs. non-intentional by people, whereas the video at the bottom of the table are the videos where the observed behaviors are not readily and successfully interpreted. Note that the first 60 video pairs are easily classifiable, with >90% of the subjects readily assessing the intentionality of the agents. These videos are used in Experiment 1. The behaviors shown in the last 20 videos in Table S1 are much less clear to people, as evidenced by the lower agreement between subjects ($>50\%$). These video pairs plus the 20 easiest behaviors are used in Experiment 2.

2.3.3   FMRI Experiments

Subjects

Twelve right-handed subjects (7 women; mean age, 25.4 years) with normal or corrected-to-normal vision participated in the present experiment. A subject had to be eliminated because of scanner failure. Another subject fell asleep and had to also be eliminated. Experimental design. The experiment lasted about 1 h 45 min, including Experiments 1 and 2, functional localizers, and T1 anatomical and field map correction (with reverse phase encoding direction) scans. All the stimulus presentation was implemented in MATLAB using Psychtoolbox and projected onto a screen mounted in the back of scanner bore and viewed by subjects through a mirror mounted on the head coil. Video stimuli had a visual angle of $9.3° \times 5.2°$.

Experiment 1

This was a block design, with 6 runs, 20 blocks per run. Each block shows one of the video stimuli. A block lasts 8 seconds, which is followed by a 12-second blank screen. Figure 2.1(b) shows the timeline of a run. Subjects were asked to pay close attention to each video. The 60 video stimuli in this experiment were presented in the first 3 runs, then repeated in the next 3 runs in a different order. The order of the videos was randomized across participants and counterbalanced within and across runs [32]. All the videos of Experiment 1 were readily interpreted as showing an intentional or non-intentional behavior in the MTurk experiment.

Experiment 2

We used a block design, with 2 runs of 20 blocks each. In this experiment, half of the videos corresponded to behaviors that are easily interpretable by people as intentional or not. The other half of the videos are the most difficult to interpret by people. The order of the videos was randomized and counterbalanced, as in Experiment 1. The task in both experiments was to passively view the stimuli; subjects in the fMRI experiments were not given any instructions to classify the videos as intentional or not. The same subjects completed Experiments 1 and 2.

Localizers

Localizer tasks were used to identify ROIs involved in Theory of Mind (ToM) and the visual analysis of biological motion, bodies, places, faces, and characters, as well as motion-sensitive area MT+ and early visual cortex (EVC) in each participant individually. To localize ToM areas, we used the false belief, false photo method of Dodell-Feder et al. (2011). The ToM ROI was selected as all clusters showing significantly greater activation for false beliefs > false photos, including temporo-parietal junction (TPJ), precuneous, and medial frontal cortex. The biological motion ROI was defined using the stimuli and technique of [25], given by the contrast of point-light display animations performing human actions versus random movements, and restricting the voxels to be in the right posterior Superior Temporal Sulcus (pSTS), as given by the atlas of [28]. Category-selective visual areas responsive to places, bodies, faces and characters (letters) were localized with the stimuli of [95]. ROIs for each category were defined as all clusters showing significantly greater activation to the given category compared to all other categories (e.g., the places

ROI included all place-selective visual regions). For the MT4+ [97] localizer task, participants fixated at the center of the screen and passively viewed blocks of either stationary or moving random dot displays. The stimuli were full screen dot patterns, and the moving patterns alternated between concentric motion towards and away from fixation at 7.5 Hz. The motion-sensitive MT+ area was defined with a moving $>$ stationary contrast. The early visual cortex (EVC) ROI was functionally defined based on the BOLD contrast comparing all images $>$ fixation from the motion discrimination task. For each subject, this contrast was used to identify the most visually responsive areas, and then anatomical landmarks were used to guide selection of bilateral ROIs covering approximately V1–V3.

MRI parameters

The fMRI experiment was conducted at Center for Cognitive and Behavioral Brain Imaging at The Ohio State University. A Siemens 3T Prisma system with 32-channel head coil is used to acquire functional and anatomical data. Whole brain functional data is collected with the following parameters: TR: 2 s; TE: 28.4 ms; multi-band factor: 3; flip angle: 72°; slice thickness: 2 mm; voxel size: 2 mm, isotropic; matrix: 120×120; FOV, 240×240 mm, yielding 72 axial slices. T1-weighted anatomical scan (MPRAGE) is collected with the following parameters: TR: 1.9 s; TE: 4.4 ms; flip angle: 12°; slice thickness: 1 mm; voxel size: 1 mm, isotropic; matrix: 176×224; FOV: 176×224 mm, which yields 256 axial slices.

2.3.4 Data analysis

We used a similar approach to that described in [94]. Data pre-processing. We used field map correction with blip up/blip down correction implemented in AFNI *3dQwarp* and *3dNwarpApply* function. We then applied motion correction, before aligning it with the structural volume. Linear detrending was applied on the functional data of Experiments 1 and 2 using AFNI's *3dTproject* function. Next, the data of each subject was mapped to the standard-brain MNI, using *auto_warp* and *3dNwarpApply* AFNI functions. The BOLD signal of each voxel was z-score-normalized (i.e., subtracted by mean and divided by the standard deviation). Then the entire time-course was shifted by 2 TRs to account for the delay of the hemodynamic response. Finally, the normalized BOLD signal of the four TRs within each block was computed, yielding a sample per block per subject, $\mathbf{x}_{ij}$, where i and j specify the subject and sample number, respectively.

Feature space

The sample vectors $\mathbf{x}_{ij}$ in the training set were used to compute the mean and covariance matrix of the PCA (Principal Component Analysis) transform [61]. The PCA transformed kept the first 70 PCs, corresponding to about 90% of the variance of the training data. Once the PCA transform was obtained, the training and testing samples were mapped onto the resulting PCA space [23, 71]. We call the projected PCA feature vectors $\hat{\mathbf{x}}_{ij}$.

MVPA classifier

Classification of a test sample is given by Linear Discriminant Analysis (LDA). The LDA classifier was computed using the training samples projected onto the PCA space [94]. In this approach, LDA finds the classification boundary in the PCA space that linearly separates the samples representing intentional and non-intentional behaviors. Binary classification accuracy is reported for the performance of this classifier.

Across-subject analysis

We used a leave-one-video-pair-out cross-validation procedure. This means that the samples of all subjects were used, and all the acquisitions except those corresponding to the two videos left out are used to train the MVPA classifier. The samples left out were used for testing. Recall that the videos left out show an intentional and a non-intentional behavior in a common scene. These videos generally include distinct dynamics, with one of them exhibiting an intentional behavior and the other one a non-intentional one. Because we have 60 video pairs, we repeated this leave-one-video-pair-out cross-validation procedure sixty times and then calculate the mean classification accuracy and standard error.

Between-subject analysis

Here, we used a leave-one-subject-out cross-validation procedure. This means that the samples of one subject were not used for training the LDA classifier. These left-out samples conformed the testing set. Since there are ten ways of leaving one subject out, we computed the classification accuracy of the MVPA decoder ten times and the report the mean classification accuracy and standard error.

Statistical significance

To compute statistical significance, we first estimated the distribution of the test statistics (i.e., classification accuracy) under the hypothesis that classification is at chance (i.e., null hypothesis). Thus, the null hypothesis states that the labels of the samples (i.e., whether a video shows an intentional or a non-intentional behavior) can be randomized without affecting the classification accuracy. To estimate this underlying, unknown distribution, we sampled 2,000 values by randomly permuting the labels of the images in each block. These accuracies plus that obtained using the true labels were rank-ordered. The rank order of the correctly labeled sample was divided by the number of permutation tests to yield the p value [53].

Reprojection maps

We used the data of all subjects in MNI to train the PCA+LDA classifier, then selected the 1% highest LDA coefficients. These coefficients were then reprojected back into the MNI brain using the inverse of the LDA and PCA functional mappings. These results were smoothed by a 2 mm Gaussian. Finally, the most significant large cluster (i.e., >100 voxels) was selected.

Chapter 3: Generative Theory of Mind: Learning to think about the actions of others

3.1 Introduction

The ability to think about other people's actions (i.e., mentalizing) is one of the hallmarks of human intelligence [50, 34], including thinking about highly abstract concepts like intent [113].

Recent work demonstrates the ability of Generative Adversarial Networks (GANs) to render images of never before seen scenes and objects [13, 30]. But, *are GANs also capable of modeling and rendering (i.e., mentalizing) highly abstract concepts like intentionality?*

This paper derives a first algorithm to achieve just that. Specifically, we first derive a set of loss functions and constraints that can be efficiently used in GANs to model intentional and non-intentional actions. We then demonstrate the network's ability to render (i.e., mentalize) previously unseen videos of intentional and non-intentional actions, Figure 3.1(a). And, finally, we derive an approach that allows us to recognize intent from previously unseen test videos. This is done by running the test video through the generative models of intentional and non-intentional actions backwards (i.e., from output to input) to identify the best representation of the observed action in each of the two learned models. Recognition is given by the model that is best at explaining (i.e., reconstructing) the test video, Figure 3.1(b).

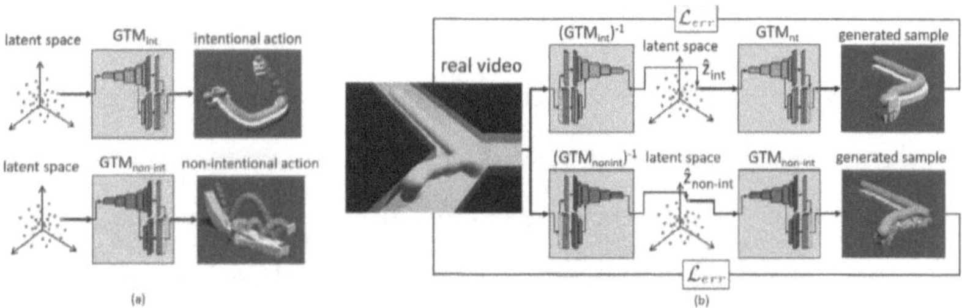

Figure 3.1: Mentalizing (theory of mind) and recognition of intentional and non-intentional actions using deep convolutional GANs. (a) Each latent vector z corresponds to an internal representation (i.e., mentalization) of either an intentional or a non-intentional action. This paper presents a first approach to learning this highly-abstract concepts of intent and non-intent. Our approach models the agent's behavior and the environment the agent interacts with, as seen in the two example outputs in this figure. The density of the blue balls is inverse proportional to its velocity. Note we model intentional and non-intentional actions using two independent networks, GAN$_{int}$ and GAN$_{non-int}$, respectively. (The discriminators of GAN$_{int}$ and GAN$_{non-int}$ are not shown. See Figure 3.2 for details.) (b) Given a test video of an action, our goal is to determine whether this action was performed intentionally or not. To do this, we run the video through the the two networks (GAN$_{int}$ and GAN$_{non-int}$) backwards, i.e., we identify the value of the latent variable z most likely to have generated this output. These z are then used to generate the videos mentalized by the intentional and non-intentional models. This shows which of the two learned models (intent or non-intent) is best at reconstructing the observed action. Comparison of our GANs' mentalized actions and the original video is given by the loss function $\mathcal{L}_{err}$.

Our GANs model the actions of an agent as well as the part of the environment it interacts with. The agent and environment are jointly modeled. But we use two networks, Figure 3.1(a). One of them is used to model and understand intentional actions. The second network models non-intentional actions. Having two models is in fact what allows us to classify any new action by simply identifying which of them best fits the observable action, Figure 3.1(b).

3.2   Related Works

A Generative Adversarial Network (GAN) is a model capable of modeling highly complex manifolds, allowing it to generate previously unseen realistic samples of the learned class [37]. GANs are composed of two modules, a discriminator and a generator (usually given as deep neural networks) which are trained under an adversarial framework [79, 67, 2]. On the one hand, a generator draws samples from an estimated distribution of the variables of interest. On the other hand, a discriminator is trained to distinguish the faked, generated samples from the true (real) ones. A minimax optimization approach in a 2-player, zero-sum game is used for learning [37]. As it is common, we will borrow the main ideas of Wasserstein GAN [9] to make the training of a GAN more stable.

A related approach to ours is that of estimating new frames of a short video clip [64, 106, 56, 112] as well as generating additional intermediate ones [47]. These papers demonstrated that given a function $f(t)$ with known values $t \in [1, T]$, GANs can estimate the value of that function in $[T + 1, T + a]$, for some small constant a; or, similarly, given the values in $t = \{1, 2, 3, \ldots, T\}$, estimate the values between each pair of sample frames, e.g., $t = \{1.1, 1.2, \ldots, 1.9\}$.

The approach derived in this paper goes two steps further. We derive an algorithm that can: *i.* estimate all the values of the underlying, unknown function $f(\cdot)$ (e.g., in the interval $[1, T]$), without the need to know its values in any part of that interval; and *ii.* estimate highly abstract functional mappings modeling theory of mind, such as the concept of intentionality. This is illustrated in Figure 3.1, and a schematic of the proposed network is given in Figure 3.2.

3.3 Learning to thinking about others

3.3.1 Problem formulation

The problem is to jointly estimate the behavior of the agent and the environment it interacts with. This means we need to model the trajectory, velocity, accelaration, etc., of the movements of the agent as well as the surface of the environment the agent interacts with.

Let the agent's 3D position at time t be given by $\mathbf{a}_t = (x_t^a, y_t^a, z_t^a)^T$, where $(x, z)^T$ are the coordinates of the plane parallel to the ground and y is the vertical direction affected by gravity, Figure 3.3(a).

Let the patch of the environment the agent interacts with at time t be $\mathbf{e}_t = (\mathbf{c}_t, \mathbf{n}_t)^T$, with $\mathbf{c}_t = (x_t^c, y_t^c, z_t^c)^T$ the 3D coordinates of the location of the surface patch and $\mathbf{n}_t = (x_t^n, y_t^n, z_t^n)^T$ its normal, $\|\mathbf{n}_t\|_2 = 1$.

Let $\mathbf{A} = (\mathbf{a}_1, \ldots, \mathbf{a}_T)^T$ be the vector defining the action of the agent, with T the total time (or image frames). Similarly, let $\mathbf{E} = (\mathbf{c}_1, \mathbf{n}_1, \ldots, \mathbf{c}_T, \mathbf{n}_T)^T$ be the vector that defines the environment the agent interacts with.

The goal is to model $\mathbf{M} = (\mathbf{A}, \mathbf{E})^T \in \mathbb{R}^{9T}$. Specifically, we want to model intentional actions, namely $\mathbf{M}_{int}$, and non-intentional actions, $\mathbf{M}_{non-int}$.

We use GANs to estimate the manifolds of intentional and non-intentional actions in $\mathbb{R}^{9T}$. These manifolds define two functional mappings, $f_{int} : \mathbb{R}^{9T} \to V$ and $f_{non-int} : \mathbb{R}^{9T} \to V$, where V is a video of either an intentional or not intentional action.

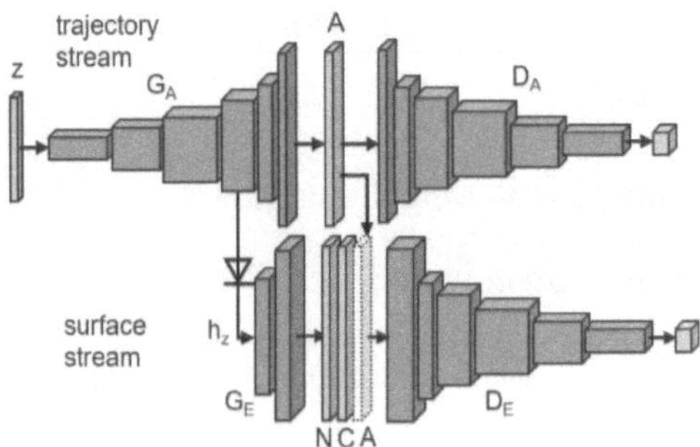

Figure 3.2: Schematic of the proposed network. The diode symbol indicates the gradient from the surface pathway does not propagate backwards to the trajectory stream.

This problem is challenging because these functional mappings are expected to be more complex than those defining images of objects and scenes. In this paper, we derive two loss functions (and associated constraints) that allow us to overcome this difficulty and achieve highly accurate modelings and simulations of intentional and non-intentional actions.

3.3.2 Derivation of the loss functions

We factor the joint distribution of $\mathbf{M}$ as $p(\mathbf{M}) = p(\mathbf{A})p(\mathbf{E}|\mathbf{A})$. That is, the modeling of the environment is dependent on the actions of the agent. This is because the agent's trajectory determines the areas of the environment that need to be modeled and rendered.

We compute $p(\mathbf{A})$ by optimizing an unconditional adversarial loss [37] that maps latent vectors $\mathbf{z} \in \mathbb{R}^q$ to $\mathbf{A}$, Figure 3.2.

We compute $p(\mathbf{E}|\mathbf{A})$ by optimizing a conditional adversarial loss [66]. This yields the mapping from an intermediate representation $\mathbf{h_z}$ of $\mathbf{A}$ to $\mathbf{E}$, Figure 3.2.

More specifically, let $\mathbf{z}$ be a latent noise vector drawn from a multivariate Normal distribution. The agent's adversarial loss is given by,

$$\mathcal{L}_A = \mathbb{E}_{\mathbf{A} \sim p_{\mathbf{A}}}[\log D_A(\mathbf{A})] + $$
$$\mathbb{E}_{\mathbf{z} \sim p_{\mathbf{z}}}[\log (1 - D_A(G_A(\mathbf{z})))], \tag{3.1}$$

where G_A is the generator, D_A is the discriminator, and the optimization is $\min_{G_A} \max_{D_A}$.

Similarly, the joint agent and surface adversarial loss is given by,

$$\mathcal{L}_M = \mathbb{E}_{\mathbf{M} \sim p_{\mathbf{M}}}[\log D_M(\mathbf{M})] + $$
$$\mathbb{E}_{\mathbf{z} \sim p_{\mathbf{z}}}[\log (1 - D_M(G_A(\mathbf{z}), G_E(\mathbf{h_z})))], \tag{3.2}$$

with the same notation as above, and $\mathbf{h_z}$ the hidden representation of the the modeling of A, Figure 3.2.

To avoid saturation, the generator is trained to maximize $\log D_A(G_A(\mathbf{z}))$ instead [37].

Recently, the Earth Mover's loss has been found to yield more stable results to the adversarial loss [9]. We have experimented with it and found it to be indeed more stable, but generally yielding equally good results in our problem. For simplicity of presentation, we will use the adversarial loss, but note that our method works with both.

3.3.3 Modeling intentional actions

The loss functions defined above can model any type of behavior, even those that do not obey the laws of physics or the physical limitations of an agent.

We define additional functions to constrain the space of possible solutions.

Roughness Term. An agent performing an intentional action generally moves in a smooth trajectory, due to the limitations imposed by internal and external forces. This introduces a penalty on the magnitude of the acceleration (based on Newton's second law).

We formulate this limitation as a roughness constraint loss $\mathcal{L}_r$ given by

$$\mathcal{L}_r = \mathbb{E}_{\mathbf{z} \sim p_{\mathbf{z}}}[r(G_A(\mathbf{z}))], \tag{3.3}$$

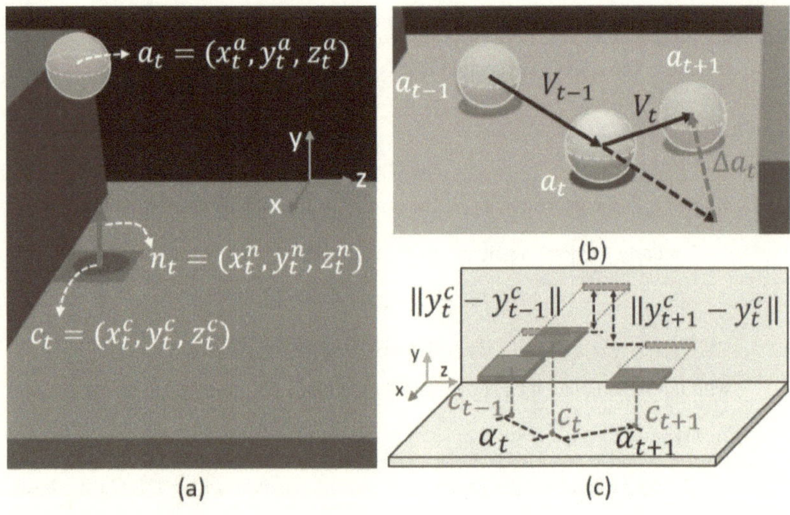

Figure 3.3: (a) Definition of $\mathbf{a}_t$, $\mathbf{c}_t$, $\mathbf{n}_t$, and world coordinate system. (b) Roughness constraint; a sharp turn yields a large $\|\Delta\mathbf{acc}_t\|_2$. (c) Spatial consistency constraint.

with the roughness measurement function $r(\mathbf{A}) : \mathbb{R}^{3T} \to \mathbb{R}$ equal to

$$\left[\sum_{t=2}^{T-1} \|\Delta\mathbf{acc}_t\|_2^2\right]^{\frac{1}{2}}, \tag{3.4}$$

$$\Delta\mathbf{acc}_t = \mathbf{a}_{t-1} - 2\mathbf{a}_t + \mathbf{a}_{t+1}, \tag{3.5}$$

where $\Delta\mathbf{acc}_t$ computes the acceleration, based on a second order finite difference, Figure 3.3(b). Of course, this constraint can also be applied to $\mathbf{E}$.

Surface patch to agent constraint. In generally, the surface patch will be close to the position of the agent, i.e., it generally makes no sense to render a scene that's away from the action performed by the agent. This can be readily modeled as,

$$\mathcal{L}_{C2A} = \mathbb{E}_{\mathbf{h_z} \sim p_{\mathbf{h_z}}} ||\mathbf{A} - G_C(\mathbf{h_z})||_p, \tag{3.6}$$

where $|| \cdot ||_p$ specifies the p-norm. Note that this term's aim is to optimize $p(\mathbf{E}|\mathbf{A})$.

Velocity to normal constraint. The orientation of the surface is also subject to physical constraints. The surface should not be oriented to block the direction of movement of the agent, i.e., the agent is not allowed to go unimpeded through walls. Formally, the angle between the velocity and the normal of the surface patches should not be greater than $90°$. That is,

$$\mathcal{L}_{V2N} = \mathbb{E}_{\mathbf{h_z} \sim p_{\mathbf{h_z}}} \sum_{t=1}^{T-1} \min \left(\widehat{\mathbf{V}}_t^T \left[\widehat{G}_N(\mathbf{h_z}) \right]_t, 0 \right), \tag{3.7}$$

where $\left[\widehat{G}_N(\mathbf{h_z}) \right]_t = \mathbf{n}^T$, $\widehat{\mathbf{V}} \in \mathbb{R}^{(T-1) \times 3}$ is the normalized matrix of the velocity matrix $\mathbf{V}$ whose t^{th} row is given by,

$$\mathbf{V}_t^T = \hat{\mathbf{a}}_{t+1}^T - \hat{\mathbf{a}}_t^T, \tag{3.8}$$

where $G_A(\mathbf{z}) = (\mathbf{a}_1, \ldots, \mathbf{a}_T)^T$, and $\hat{\mathbf{a}}_t = \mathbf{a}_t / ||\mathbf{a}_t||_2$.

Spatial consistency constraint. We assume that the height (y coordinate) of the scene varies gradually most of the time, i.e., discontinuities (which may define changes between surfaces of different objects) are less common than smooth changing surfaces. For example, a table has a smooth surface and a discontinuity occurs only around its edges, when the agent moves from the table to the floor.

We define this formally as,

$$\mathcal{L}_{SC} = \mathbb{E}_{\mathbf{h_z} \sim p_{\mathbf{h_z}}} \left[(T-1)^{-1} \sum_{t=2}^{T} \alpha_t \left\| [G_C(\mathbf{h_z})]_{yt} - [G_C(\mathbf{h_z})]_{y(t-1)} \right\|_p \right], \tag{3.9}$$

where $[G_C(\mathbf{h_z})]_{yt} = y_t^c$ is the y coordinate at time t of the vector $\mathbf{c}_t$ generated by $G_C(\cdot)$,

$$\alpha_t = \left\| [G_C(\mathbf{h_z})]_{(x,z)t} - [G_C(\mathbf{h_z})]_{(x,z)(t-1)} \right\|_2^{-1} \tag{3.10}$$

is the inverse of the Euclidean distance on the x, z-plane between the patches computed at time t and $t - 1$ (the closer the two patches, the higher the weight), $[G_C(\mathbf{h_z})]_{(x,z)t} = (x_t^c, z_t^c)^T$, Figure 3.3(c).

Agent on top of the surface constraint. Since we are only rendering the surface defining the part of the scene the agent moves over to, the y coordinate of the agent must be greater or equal to that of the surface. Formally,

$$\mathcal{L}_P = \mathbb{E}_{\mathbf{z} \sim p_{\mathbf{z}}} \left[T^{-1} \sum_{t=1}^{T} \beta_t \left\| \min \left([G_A(\mathbf{z})]_{yt} - [G_C(\mathbf{h_z})]_{yt}, 0 \right) \right\|_p \right], \tag{3.11}$$

where $\beta_{ij} = \left\| [G_A(\mathbf{z})]_{(x,z)t} - [G_C(\mathbf{h_z})]_{(x,z)t} \right\|_2^{-1}$ is the inverse Euclidean distance between the agent location and path location on the x, z-plane at time t.

Notice that the use of the function $\min(\cdot, 0)$ means we only penalize for surfaces that are above the agent.

Intentional actions loss. The loss of intentional actions is given by the weighted sum of the adversarial loss and the additional constraints derived above. That is,

$$\mathcal{L}_{int} = \lambda_A \mathcal{L}_A + \lambda_M \mathcal{L}_M + \lambda_r \mathcal{L}_r + \lambda_{C2A} \mathcal{L}_{C2A} + \lambda_{V2N} \mathcal{L}_{V2N} + \lambda_{SC} \mathcal{L}_{SC} + \lambda_P \mathcal{L}_P. \tag{3.12}$$

3.3.4 Non-intentional constraints

A non-intentional action must abide by Newton's laws. We derive a set of constraints to better define the subspace of $p_{\mathbf{z}}$ associated to non-intentional actions.

Conservation of the total energy of the system. Agents have a hidden internal engine that allow them to move in a way that seems to add or subtract energy from the system. Of course, this is only an illusion, since the total energy of the system must be preserved. It's an illusion because the energy generated by the agent is non-observable.

But, non-intentional actions must preserved the *observed* mechanical (i.e., kinetic + potential) energy of the system.

One challenge to estimating this conservation of energy is that the actions generated by GANs are normalized to fit the range of the *tanh* function. This introduces a scaling ambiguity. This scaling factor leaves the gravitational constant undetermined, which means that the total energy of the system may not be computable.

To solve this limitation, we derive a scale invariant measure of the energy term. Let $\mathcal{T}_t$ denotes the total energy at frame t. Then, the following holds,

$$\mathcal{T}_t = \frac{1}{2} m \left\| \mathbf{V}_t \right\|^2 + mg \left[G_A(\mathbf{z}) \right]_{yt}, \tag{3.13}$$

where m is the mass of the object and g is the gravitational constant.

Since the total energy is preserved over time, we have

$$\mathcal{T}_{t-1} = \mathcal{T}_t = \mathcal{T}_{t+1}. \tag{3.14}$$

Combining (3.13) and (3.14) yields

$$\frac{1}{2} m (\left\| \mathbf{V}_t \right\|^2 - \left\| \mathbf{V}_{t-1} \right\|^2) = mg([G_A(\mathbf{z})]_{y(t-1)} - [G_A(\mathbf{z})]_{yt}) \tag{3.15}$$

$$\frac{1}{2} m (\left\| \mathbf{V}_{t+1} \right\|^2 - \left\| \mathbf{V}_t \right\|^2) = mg([G_A(\mathbf{z})]_{yt} - [G_A(\mathbf{z})]_{y(t+1)}). \tag{3.16}$$

When (3.16) in non-zero, we have

$$\frac{\left\| \mathbf{V}_t \right\|^2 - \left\| \mathbf{V}_{t-1} \right\|^2}{\left\| \mathbf{V}_{t+1} \right\|^2 - \left\| \mathbf{V}_t \right\|^2} - \frac{[G_A(\mathbf{z})]_{y(t-1)} - [G_A(\mathbf{z})]_{yt}}{[G_A(\mathbf{z})]_{yt} - [G_A(\mathbf{z})]_{y(t+1)}} = 0. \tag{3.17}$$

Thus, the minimization of the following constraint guarantees the total mechanical energy is maintained over time,

$$\mathcal{L}_T = \sum_{t=2}^{T-1} \left| \left(\|\mathbf{V}_t\|^2 - \|\mathbf{V}_{t-1}\|^2 \right) \left([G_A(\mathbf{z})]_{yt} - [G_A(\mathbf{z})]_{y(t+1)} \right) - \left(\|\mathbf{V}_{t+1}\|^2 - \|\mathbf{V}_t\|^2 \right) \left([G_A(\mathbf{z})]_{y(t-1)} - [G_A(\mathbf{z})]_{y(t)} \right) \right|. \tag{3.18}$$

Constant vertical acceleration constraint. The only external force acting on an object (or agent) moving non-intentionally is gravity. This means that the vertical acceleration of the object should be constant everywhere since the object is either on the ground or in free fall.

More formally, the constant vertical acceleration can be written as the minimization of

$$\mathcal{L}_G = \Delta \left[G_A(\mathbf{z})\right]_{yt}. \tag{3.19}$$

Non-intentional actions loss. We now use the results derived above to define our loss function for non-intentional actions. This loss is for the GAN that models non-intentional actions. It is given by

$$\begin{aligned}
\mathcal{L}_{non-int} = & \lambda_A \mathcal{L}_A + \lambda_M \mathcal{L}_M + \lambda_r \mathcal{L}_r + \lambda_{C2T} \mathcal{L}_{C2A} + \\
& \lambda_{V2N} \mathcal{L}_{V2N} \lambda_{SC} \mathcal{L}_{SC} + \lambda_P \mathcal{L}_P + \lambda_T \mathcal{L}_T + \\
& \lambda_G \mathcal{L}_G.
\end{aligned} \tag{3.20}$$

3.4 Mentalizing with GANs

In this section, we define the details of the architecture and parameters used by our algorithm.

3.4.1 Network design

Our network is a Deep Convolutional GAN (DCGAN) [79]. In recent years, DCGANs have been successfully used to model scenes and objects, with increasingly realistic results [22, 77, 55]. DCGANs have also been used for image "translation," e.g., to find the mapping of a drawing to some corresponding color image [46], or change the attributes of an image [7]. And similar networks have been successfully used to model and render the scene an agent interacts with [30].

We model intentional and non-intentional actions separately, using two independent DCGANs. That is, we use a first network, GAN_{int}, to model the behavior of an agent and its interaction with the environment when this agent moves intentionally, $\mathbf{M}_{int}$. And, we use a second network, $\text{GAN}_{non-int}$, to model the movement of an object (or agent) caused by the laws of physics, i.e., a non-intentional movement and the accompanying environment, $\mathbf{M}_{non-int}$.

Each of these networks is further divided into two parts, Figure 3.2. The top part (as seen in the figure) models the behavior of the agent, $G_A(\cdot)$. The bottom part of the network models the area of the environment the agent interacts with, $G_E(\cdot) = (G_C(\cdot), G_N(\cdot))$.

Note that the hidden representation of the top network, $\mathbf{h_z}$, is the vector that conditions the bottom network, resulting in a conditional GAN [66]. The reason for this is as follows. The generator of the environment, $G_E(\cdot)$, must render the areas of the scene the agent interacts with. That means that this generator must know what the generator of the agent, $G_A(\cdot)$, is modeling. For example, is the patch of the scene to be rendered part of the ground (x, z-plane)? Or, is it part of a wall the agent is bouncing off (y-axis)?

The discriminators, $D_A(\cdot)$ and $D_E(\cdot)$, are mirror images of the generators, as shown in Figure 3.2.

3.4.2 Implementation details

Agent generator, G_A. Similar to [106, 79], we use fractionally-strided convolutions to perform up-sampling in the agent's generator G_A to map from a noise vector $\mathbf{z} \in \mathbb{R}^d$ to $\mathbf{A}$.

We use a 6-layer network with kernel size $= 6 \times 3$, stride $= 2$, and padding $= 2$, except for the first layer, which uses kernel size $= 8 \times 3$ with stride $= 1$ and padding $= 0$. This specific set of parameters is chosen so that the duration of the generated trajectory is sufficiently long ($T = 256$) to represent a complete intentional or non-intentional action.

Discriminator of the agent's trajectory, D_A. This is a 6-layer convolutional neural network taking either the generated trajectories or some real observed actions as input.

Here, we use a regular convolution kernel of size $= 6 \times 3$, with stride $= 2$ and padding $= 2$, except for the last layer which has kernel size $= 8 \times 3$, stride $= 1$, and padding $= 0$.

Environment generator, G_E. This generator takes the hidden representation $\mathbf{h_z}$ of the agent's trajectory as a condition to generate the patch of the environment the agent is interacting with. $\mathbf{h_z}$ is the hidden representation given by the 4th layer of G_A. These are, thus, the deep features used to represent the behavior of the agent.

The architecture of G_E is the same as the last two layers in G_A, except for the obvious fact that it has twice as many outputs, $\mathbf{C}$ and $\mathbf{N}$. Similar to [46], we do not explicitly include latent noise as an additional input.

Environment discriminator, D_E. This discriminator uses the agent's trajectory as well as the 3D position and orientation of the patch the agent is interacting with as inputs, $\mathbf{M}$. This discriminator uses the same architecture as D_A, with the obvious difference that it has more input dimensions.

3.4.3 Experimental details

In our experimental results reported below, we use $d = 50$. This means we draw z from a Normal distribution defined in $\mathbb{R}^{50}$.

To train the intentional model, we use the following parameters: $\lambda_A = 2$, $\lambda_M = 2$, $\lambda_r = 2$, $\lambda_{C2A} = 20$, $\lambda_{V2N} = 20$, $\lambda_{SC} = 20$, $\lambda_P = 5$.

We train the non-intentional model with the following parameters: $\lambda_A = 2$, $\lambda_M = 2$, $\lambda_r = 2$, $\lambda_{C2A} = 10$, $\lambda_{V2N} = 20$, $\lambda_{SC} = 30$, $\lambda_P = 5$, $\lambda_T = 10^4$, $\lambda_G = 50$.

We use Adam [49] to optimize the parameters of both networks, GAN_{int} and $\text{GAN}_{non-int}$. The initial learning rate = .0002, $\beta_1 = .5$, and $\beta_2 = .999$. We train each model on 100K iterations. And, we use a batch size = 64.

Both, the discriminator and generator, are trained once per iteration. We found no significant improvement when balancing the training of the discriminator and the generator. Each model takes about 4 hours to train on a workstation with Intel Core i7-8700K and a NVIDIA GTX 1080Ti.

3.5 Visual Recognition of Intent

We now derive an approach to classify a novel test video, not previously observed by either network, as showing an intentional or a non-intentional action.

Note that GAN_{int} has learned an estimate of the manifold of intentional actions. Similarly, $\text{GAN}_{non-int}$ has learned the manifold of non-intentional actions.

Given a previously unseen action, we wish to determine whether it is best described by the manifold defining intentional actions or by the one describing non-intentional actions.

This can be achieved by reversing the mapping function defining each manifold. That is, we want to find the the latent variable z that may generate such an observation. The key to this process is to realize that this is the same as mentalizing the action first as intentional and then as non-intentional to see which model best fits the observation.

Although the networks GAN_{int} and $\text{GAN}_{non-int}$ define highly non-linear and non-invertible functions, we can employ an optimization algorithm to find a solution.

Formally, given a testing sample $\mathbf{M}_{test} = (\mathbf{A}_{test}, \mathbf{E}_{test})^T$, we wish to find the value of the latent variable $\hat{\mathbf{z}}$ that minimizes a fitting function. This is given by,

$$\hat{\mathbf{z}} = \arg\min_{\mathbf{z}} \mathcal{L}_{err}\left(G_M(\mathbf{z}), \mathbf{M}_{test}\right), \tag{3.21}$$

where the fitting function $\mathcal{L}_{err}\left(G_M(\mathbf{z}), \mathbf{M}_{test}\right)$ is defined as

$$\mathcal{L}_{err}(G_M(\mathbf{z}), \mathbf{M}_{test}) = \kappa \left\|G_A(\mathbf{z}) - \mathbf{A}_{test}\right\|_2 + \\ \left\|G_E(\mathbf{h_z}) - \mathbf{E}_{test}\right\|_2, \tag{3.22}$$

and κ is a scalar controlling the importance of trajectory of the agent versus that of the surface patch.

A solution to (3.21) can be computed using gradient descent. This yields two latent variable results, $\hat{\mathbf{z}}_{int}$ and $\hat{\mathbf{z}}_{non-int}$. The first results is given by optimizing GAN_{int}; the second by optimizing $\text{GAN}_{non-int}$.

Now that we have $\hat{\mathbf{z}}_{int}$ and $\hat{\mathbf{z}}_{non-int}$, we need to determine which of these internal representations best describes our observation.

To do this, we mentalize (render) the videos given by each of the two networks, i.e., generate the videos using $\hat{\mathbf{z}}_{int}$ in GAN_{int} and $\hat{\mathbf{z}}_{non-int}$ in $\text{GAN}_{non-int}$. The netowk that generates the closest action and environment to the observed one wins.

Formally (see also , Figure 3.1(b)),

$$\arg\min_{i=\{int,non-int\}} \mathcal{L}_{err}(G_M(\mathbf{z}_i), \mathbf{M}_{test}). \tag{3.23}$$

The above equations only work for videos of length T. When the testing video contains a longer trajectory, one can chose to select multiple T-frame segments from the entire trajectory, run the classifier on each segment, and aggregate the result.

We use a heuristic that if at least a segment in the entire trajectory is intentional then the entire trajectory is intentional. This is due to the fact that intentional trajectories can contain segments where the agent exhibits pure Newtonian motion; for example, during an agent's free falls after a jump.

3.6 Experimental Results

We provide experimental results of the learning of the intentional and non-intentional manifolds defined by GAN_{int} and $\text{GAN}_{non-int}$, the generation of never before seen videos, and the recognition of previously unobserved videos, Figure 3.1.

3.6.1 Videos

We manually designed 60 3D animations of agents acting intentionally or non-intentionally. Our videos follow the classical model of Heider and Simmel [43] (video shown in Figure 1.1). In their paper, Heider and Simmel demonstrated that people readily interpret intent even from actions performed by abstract or geometrical objects. 30 of our videos show intentional actions. The other 30 videos show non-intentional actions. Samples videos are provided in Figure 2.2.

Videos consist of balls moving in a 3D scene during a span of 480 frames. In the intentional videos, the ball moves in a human-like manner (as in the Simmel and Heider animation discused above). In the non-intentional videos, the ball moves according to the laws of physics.

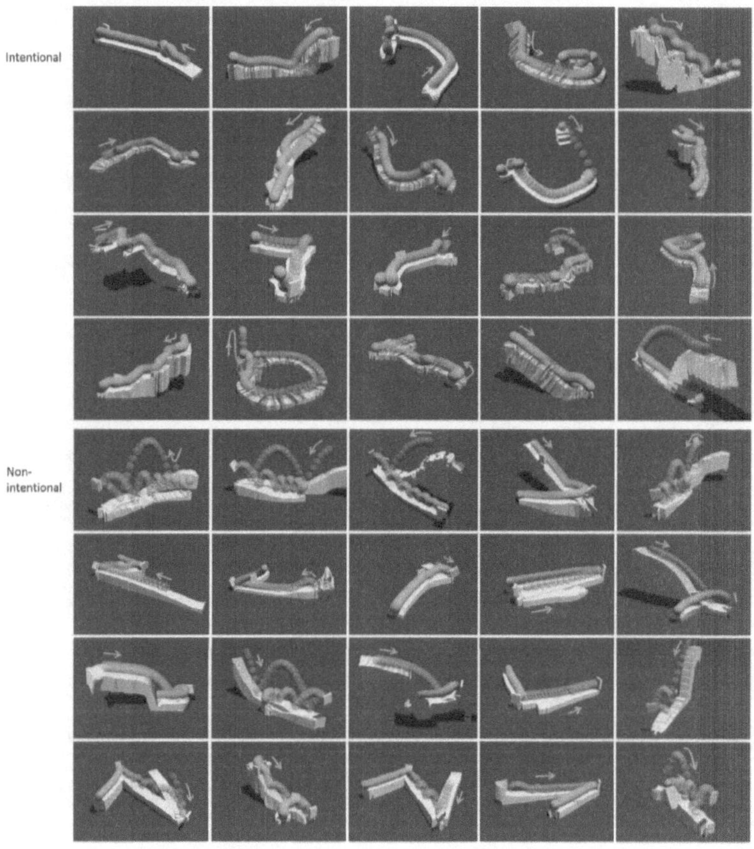

Figure 3.4: Sample videos generated by GAN_{int} and $GAN_{non-int}$ and used in our Amazon Mechanical Turk experiment. The results of this experiment are in Table 3.1. Actual videos available in Figure 3.5

.

We use the computer graphics software Maya 2015 to generate the videos. Keyframe animation is used for hand-crafting the intentional movement of the ball. Bullet Physical Engine is used to describe the Newtonian motion of the non-intentional actions.

To ensure that the videos are indeed perceived as intentional and non-intentional by people, we asked 30 Amazon Mechanical (AM) Turkers to evaluate each video. Each AM Turker judged whether the actions in the videos were intentionally or not. All videos had at least 90% agreement between AM Turkers, indicating that the videos are reliably classified as intentional/non-intentional by humans.

3.6.2 Ground truth data

The true agent trajectory $\mathbf{A}$ and corresponding surface patches are extracted from the Maya animations. All trajectory and surface patches are defined with respect to the default world coordinate in Maya.

Since we only focus on single agent, in the case of multi-agent videos, the trajectory of each agent is extracted and treated as an independent sample. To generate actions with multiple agents, we run our algorithm multiple times, each time generating the trajectory and environment of an agent.

The surface patches are selected to have: 1. the patch underneath the agent, 2. the same x, y coordinate for the patch and the agent, and 3. the smallest vertical distance from agent to patch.

After $\mathbf{A}$, $\mathbf{C}$, and $\mathbf{N}$ are obtained, we perform data augmentation on the training samples. Each trajectory is rotated about the y-axis in $5°$ increments for total $359°$. This yields a total of 72 samples per original trajectory. We also extract all the possible 256-frame-long segments from each trajectory.

3.6.3 Data Preprocessing

The trajectory is normalized to be centered around the origin and scaled by $2\max(\mathbf{A})$ where $\max(\cdot)$ is a function that returns the maximum valued element in the matrix. This normalizes the trajectory to be in the range of $tanh(\cdot)$ activation function. This is a requirement because GANs use $tanh(\cdot)$. The same normalizing factor is applied to $\mathbf{C}$.

Since the trajectory and surface center are normalized to fit into the range of the activation function, the scale of the generated sample is unknown, which leads to ambiguous surface-agent interactions.

Let the surface-agent distance $g_t = \|\mathbf{C}_t - \mathbf{A}_t\|_2$. If $g_t = r$, with r the radius of the ball, then the surface supports the agent. If $g_t > r$, the agent is in the air.

If $g_t < r$, this defines an impossible configuration. These are thus eliminated from further consideration.

3.6.4 Mentalizing: video rendering

We generated 100 videos of intentional actions and 100 videos of non-intentional actions by drawing $\mathbf{z}$ from the Normal distributions of the latent spaces in GAN_{int} and $\text{GAN}_{non-int}$, Figure 3.1.

To ensure that the trajectory of the agent generated by our GANs is in the field of view of the camera, its value is mean centered and scaled, $\tilde{\mathbf{A}} = \gamma \mathbf{A}/\|\mathbf{A}\|_F$, where $\|\cdot\|_F$ specifies the Frobenius norm.

The same normalization is applied to $\mathbf{C}$. Then, for each frame t, $\mathbf{C}_t$ is translated along the surface normal (away from the agent) by the radius of the ball. That is, $\tilde{\mathbf{C}}_t = \mathbf{C}_t - r\mathbf{N}_t$. Note that this step is in fact the inverse of the center translation performed during data preprocessing.

In all our experiments, we used $r = .1$, and $\gamma = 10$. All videos are rendered at 60 fps, 1028×686 resolution, single point light source. All objects are defined to have Lambertian bidirectional reflectance distribution functions.

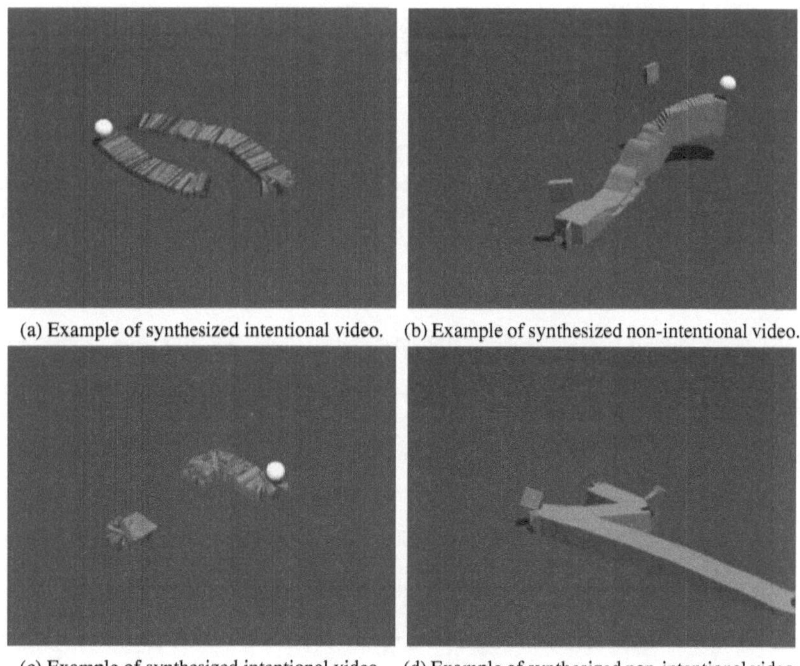

(a) Example of synthesized intentional video.	(b) Example of synthesized non-intentional video.
(c) Example of synthesized intentional video.	(d) Example of synthesized non-intentional video.

Figure 3.5: [Video] Examples of intentional and non-intentional videos generated by the proposed algorithm. Both agents' movement and environmental context are generated by our algorithm. Please click the image to play the video (Adobe Acrobat Reader required).

3.6.5 Correctness of the rendered videos

To determine the accuracy (veracity) of the GAN rendered videos, we run an online experiment in Amazon Mechanical Turk. The goal is to see whether human subjects classify the GAN's generated videos as intentional and non-intentional actions correctly.

Category	Accuracy
Intentional	100%
Non-intentional	91%

Table 3.1: Result of the Amazon Mechanical Turker experiment. Human participants are asked to labeled GAN-generated videos as showing an intentional or a non-intentional action. The table shows perceptual accuracy across Turkers.

For this test, we generate 100 videos with GAN_{int} and 100 videos with $\text{GAN}_{non-int}$. Sample videos of intentional and non-intentional actions generated by GAN_{int} and $\text{GAN}_{non-int}$ are given in Figure 3.4.

Each of the 200 generated videos is evaluated by 5 independent AM Turkers. Each human subject is asked to answer a binary-forced-choice question after watching the video. The question and submit button are not available until the video has played fully. Turkers can watch each video once or twice. We also provide two examples for each class from the hand-crafted videos. Those examples are held-out from the training set to ensure that the result is not due to low-level pattern matching.

We use majority vote to identify the perceived category for each video; if three or more Turkers voted for the correct category, the video is considered to display the correct typ of action. The results are shown in Table 3.1. As we can see in these results, there was high agreement amongst AM Turkers. This is true for both categories of videos; those showing intentional actions and those showing non-intentional actions.

3.6.6 Automatic recognition of intent

As described in Section 3.5, we can use the derived approach to recognize newly observed, test videos of actions into intentional and non-intentional actions.

To test this, we used a leave-one-pair-out cross-validation (CV) procedure, where at each CV iteration we hold a pair of videos out for testing; a video of an intentional action, and a video of a non-intentional actions.

For each testing trajectory we first extract three 256-frame trajectory segments, starting at the 1st, 101st and 201st frame. If at least one of these segments is classified as intentional, then the video is said to be showing an intentional action.

With the above defined algorithm, we obtained a classification accuracy of **79.16%** on our dataset.

Parameters. We set $\kappa = 2$. We optimize with Adam [49], with learning rate $= .0005$, $\beta_1 = .9$, and $\beta_2 = .999$. The optimization stops when the loss does not improve for 1,000 iterations or the number of iteration reaches 20K.

More details of the baseline implementation and comparison is provided in Appendix B.

Method	Accuracy
Ours	79.16%
Ours, w/o {C2A}	62.50%
Ours, w/o {r}	60.42%
Ours, w/o {V2N}	58.33%
Ours, w/o {SC}	56.25%
Ours, w/o {P}	56.25%
Ours, w/o {C2A, r}	56.25%
Ours, w/o {C2A, r, V2N}	56.25%
Ours, w/o regualrizers	58.33%

Table 3.2: Ablation study. Ours: GTM model with full loss. Ours w/o **x**: **x** is removed from the loss function during training.

3.6.7 Ablation Study

To study the contribution of each regularizer term, an ablation study is conducted on the proposed model. Table 3.2 shows the results of the ablation study. Starting with the GTM of Section 3.5, we gradually remove each regularizer, to determine their individual contribution. The model is then trained with the ablated loss and evaluated using cross-validation.

3.7 Conclusions

We have presented the first algorithm able to render video clips of intentional and non-intentional actions from a single (noise) latent variable z. We demonstrated our approach's ability to generate videos of the highly-abstract concept of intentionality with amazing fidelity, Table 3.1 and Figure 3.4. We have also shown how we can apply the derived algorithm to classify previously unseen actions as intentional or not.

Chapter 4: Interpreting People's Intents and Answering

Counterfactuals

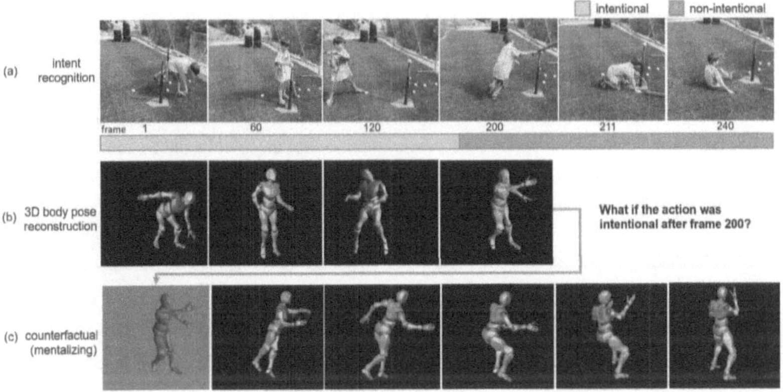

Figure 4.1: (a) A video of a kid playing with a T-ball set: a child picks up a ball from the floor and places it on top of the set intentionally, before trying to bat and falling to the ground unintentionally. We derive a computer vision algorithm to identify which actions are performed intentional and which non-intentionally. (b) 3D body pose recovery of the actions of the kid in the video in (a). (c) A possible answer to a hypothetical question (a counterfactual) on what would have been the kid's action had he not fallen to the ground but, rather, completed the swing successfully.

4.1 Introduction

Consider the actions observed in Figure 1(a). To us, this video clearly starts with a set

of intentional actions, before turning into a non-intentional fall after frame 200. We know

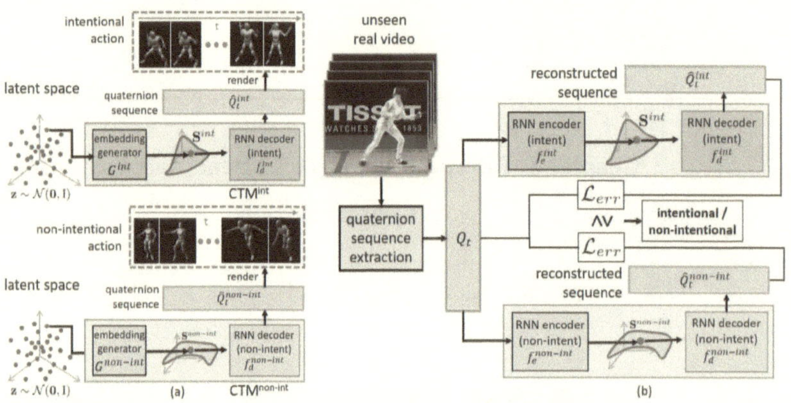

Figure 4.2: (a) Schematic of the proposed framework, Computational Theory of Mind (CTM). Each latent vector **z** corresponds to either an intentional or a non-intentional action. We derive an algorithm to estimate the underlying distribution of intentional (CTM^{int}) and non-intentional (CTM$^{non-int}$) actions. (b) The action in a test video is classified as intentional if the latent variable that best represents it is closer to the distribution of intentional actions than to that of non-intentional actions.

this because we can reason about the actions of others [113]. This human ability is called *theory of mind*, and the faculty to think about what may happen to others under some non-observable, hypothetical conditions is called *mentalizing* [50, 34]. Humans use theory of mind to identify whether an observed action was done intentionally or not, and to ask and answer hypothetical questions like "what would have happen if ...?" The ability to ask and answer these counterfactuals (i.e., "what ifs") has been noted as one of the most complex achievements of human intelligence [73].

Here, we derive, to our knowledge, the first algorithm able to perform these high-level human tasks. Specifically, we first derive an algorithm that can be efficiently used to model intentional and non-intentional actions. In our framework, the goal is to learn the underlying distribution of intentional and non-intentional actions in some latent space. We refer to the resulting algorithm that achieves this as Computational Theory of Mind (CTM).

Second, we demonstrate CTM's ability to render (i.e., mentalize) previously unseen videos of intentional and non-intentional actions, Figure 4.1(b-c). This is done by generating the video of samples drawn from the learned distribution of intent and non-intent in the latent space, 4.2(a). This ability to render never-seen videos allows us to answer counterfactuals, Figure 4.1(c).

And, crucially, the derived algorithm allows us to recognize intent from previously unseen test videos. This is done by running the test video through the learned models of intentional and non-intentional actions to identify the best latent space representation of the observed action. Recognition is given by the model that is best at explaining (i.e., reconstructing) the test video, Figure 4.2(b).

The proposed CTM is divided into two modules, Figure 4.2. The first is used to mentalize and visually recognize intentional actions. The second models non-intentional actions. We will referr to them as, CTM^{int} and $CTM^{non-int}$, respectively.

4.1.1 Related works

The DNNs most related to our work are Generative Adversarial Networks (GANs). A GAN is a model capable of modeling highly complex manifolds, allowing it to generate previously unseen realistic samples of the learned class [37]. GANs are composed of two modules, a discriminator and a generator (usually given as deep neural networks) which are trained under an adversarial framework [79, 67, 2]. On the one hand, a generator draws samples from an estimated distribution of the variables of interest ad generates new fake samples. On the other hand, a discriminator is trained to distinguish these fake samples from the true ones. A minimax optimization approach in a 2-player, zero-sum game is used for learning [37].

Another related approach to ours is that of estimating new frames of a short video clip [64, 106, 56, 112] as well as generating additional intermediate ones [47]. These papers demonstrated that given a function $f(t)$ with known values $t \in [1, T]$, DNNs can estimate the value of that function in $[T + 1, T + a]$, for some small constant a; or, similarly, given the values in $t = \{1, 2, 3, \ldots, T\}$, estimate the values between each pair of sample frames, e.g., $t = \{1.1, 1.2, \ldots, 1.9\}$.

The approach derived in this paper goes two steps further. We derive an algorithm that can:

1. estimate all the values of the underlying, unknown function $f(\cdot)$ (e.g., in the interval $[1, T]$), *without the need to know its values at any point in this interval*;

2. *estimate highly abstract functional mappings modeling theory of mind, such as the concept of intentionality.* This is illustrated in Figure 4.1, and a schematic of the proposed network is given in Figure 4.2.

4.2 Thinking about the actions of others

4.2.1 Problem formulation

Given a never-before-seen video of the behavior of a person, can we derive a computer vision algorithm that recognizes if her actions are performed intentionally? And, once this inference is achieved, can we answer counterfactuals of the observed action?

In this paper, we show that the above questions can be answered in the affirmative. Furthermore, we demonstrate we can make this inference from the person's kinematics alone.

Although highly abstract, numerous psychological and neuroscience studies demonstrate that people can readily identify intentionality and answer counterfactuals from their kinematic information alone [12, 48, 43, 15].

4.2.2 Model of the kinematics

We represent human actions using the kinematics of a person's body joints, discarding all the shading and contextual information in the video.

Joint movements can be parametrized using the person's joint rotation [72, 118]. Modeling the rotation of each joint provides a representation with a low number of degrees-of-freedom that is invariant to whole-body translation, rotation, scale, and the world- and camera-coordinate systems.

Hence, we represent the human action as a temporal sequences of joint rotations. Similar to [72], we use unit quaternions to paramatrize the joint rotation due to their advantage in continuity and because they are free of singularities, which is not the case when we use Euler angles.

Let the rotation of the ith joint at time t be given by the quaternion $q_t^i = w_t^i + x_t^i \mathbf{i} + y_t^i \mathbf{j} + z_t^i \mathbf{k}$, with $w_t^{i^2} + x_t^{i^2} + y_t^{i^2} + z_t^{i^2} = 1$, for $\forall i, t$, and $\mathbf{q}_t^i = (w_t^i, x_t^i, y_t^i, z_t^i)^\top$ its vector representation in $\mathbb{R}^4$.

The human pose at frame t can be defined as a matrix $\mathbf{Q}_t \in \mathbb{R}^{d \times 4}$, $\mathbf{Q}_t = (\mathbf{q}_t^1, \mathbf{q}_t^2, \ldots, \mathbf{q}_t^d)^\top$, where d is the number of joints of in the skeleton template used to represent the human body. The action of the human agent can then be defined by the sequence $\{\mathbf{Q}_1, \mathbf{Q}_2, \ldots, \mathbf{Q}_T\}$, or more compactly $\mathcal{Q} = \{\mathbf{Q}_t : t \in \{1, 2, \ldots, T\}\}$, with T the total time (or number of image frames).

Our goal is to model the underlying distributions $\mathbf{Q}^{int}$ and $\mathbf{Q}^{non-int}$ of intentional and non-intentional actions in latent space. Then, given a new test observation $\mathcal{Q}$, we can readily determine to which of these two distributions each $\mathbf{Q}_t$ is closest, yielding a classification of each video frame into either intentional or not, Figure 4.1(a).

The following sections will derive the method for modeling the underlying distribution of $\mathbf{Q}^{int}$. The same formulation applies to the modeling of $\mathbf{Q}^{non-int}$, with a specific treatment of the small (non-intentional actions) sample problem given in Section 4.2.5.

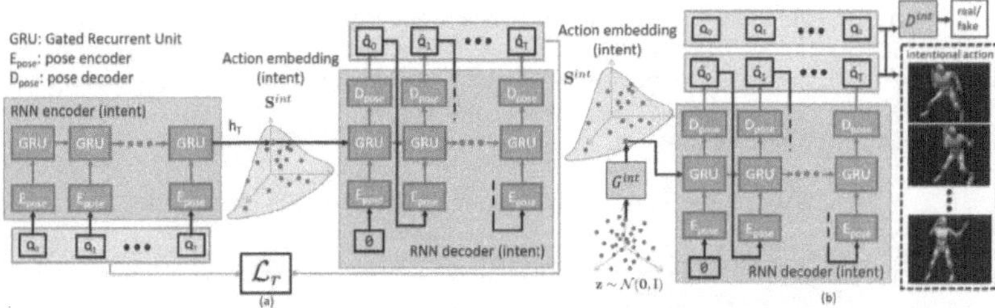

Figure 4.3: (a) Schematic of the network used to learn the embedding of intentional actions (encoder), and the decoder used to generate fake (mentalized) videos (b). The same applies to the network that models non-intentional actions.

4.2.3 Using an embedding space

The space of all possible quaternions defines all possible rotations of every joint. Not all of these movements are humanly possible, i.e., they either have physically implausible joint angle configuration, or non-smooth pose transition across frames. Thus, we propose to learn two lower dimensional embeddings, $\mathbf{S}^{int}$ and $\mathbf{S}^{non-int}$, which define only plausible human body movements.

Formally, let $f_e^{int} : \mathcal{Q} \to \mathbf{S}^{int}$ be the function that maps an intentional human action to its embedding space (that is, of course, the encoder), with $\mathbf{S}^{int} \subseteq \mathbb{R}^m$. Similarly, let $f_d^{int} : \mathbf{S}^{int} \to \mathcal{Q}$ be the mapping from the embedding space to a plausible intentional human action (i.e., decoder).

We learn these functional mappings by minimizing the reconstruction error loss; formally,

$$\mathcal{L}_r = \frac{1}{N}\frac{1}{T}\sum_{k=1}^{N}\sum_{t=1}^{T}\left\|\mathbf{Q}_{kt} - f_d^{int}(f_e^{int}(\mathbf{Q}_{kt}))\right\|_{\mathrm{F}}^2 , \tag{4.1}$$

where $\|.\|_{\mathrm{F}}$ is the Frobenius norm, $\mathcal{Q}_k = \{\mathbf{Q}_{k1}, \ldots, \mathbf{Q}_{kT}\}$ is the kth sample, $k = 1, \ldots, N$, N is the total number of samples, and we use two Recurrent Neural Network (RNN), one to model f_e^{int} and another for f_d^{int}.

The details of this model are in Figure 4.3. As we see in this figure, the proposed encoder-decoder models the kinematics of a plausible human action, which is what we were set out to do, as defined in Section 4.2.2.

Using the encoder in the proposed model allows us to represent any intentional and non-intentional action as a vector of this embedding, Figure 4.2(a). And, we can use the decoder to generate (i.e., mentalize) new plausible intentional and non-intentional human actions by decoding vectors of the embedding, Figures 4.2(a) and 4.3(b).

4.2.4 Finding the underlying distribution

The intentional and non-intentional embedding spaces $\mathbf{S}^{int}$ and $\mathbf{S}^{non-int}$ are compact representation of plausible intentional and non-intentional human actions.

We now wish to refine this representation, i.e., identify the distributions in $\mathbf{S}^{int}$ and $\mathbf{S}^{non-int}$ that most accurately represent intentional and non-intentional human actions, and not those that seem slightly off target.

To better understand this, consider an embedding space that represents images of human faces. In that case, we would want to find the underlying distribution of vectors that, when decoded, generate photo-realistic face images that are indistinguishable from pictures of actual faces.

Similarly, our goal, is to find the underlying distributions in $\mathbf{S}^{int}$ and $\mathbf{S}^{non-int}$ that generate human actions that look as realistic as possible. This is exactly what Generative Adversarial Network (GAN) do. Thus, we use a GAN to uncover these underlying distributions. Although the GAN does not provide explicit modeling on the distribution, it provides sampling according to the distribution.

Let the generator of the GAN modeling intentional actions in $\mathbf{S}^{int}$ be $G^{int} : \mathbf{z} \rightarrow \mathbf{S}^{int}$, where $\mathbf{z} \sim \mathcal{N}(0, \mathrm{I})$, which maps vectors sampled from a zero-mean, unit-variance multivariate Normal distribution to the intentional embedding and, hence, implicitly models the underlying distribution function of intentional actions, $p_{int} \in \mathbf{S}^{int}$.

The discriminator is defined as $D^{int} : \mathcal{Q} \rightarrow \mathbb{R}$, where $\mathcal{Q}$ can either be a sequence generated by our model (denoted $\widehat{\mathcal{Q}}$, Figure 4.3(b)), or a sequence of a real video from a training set $\mathcal{X} = \{\mathcal{Q}_k\}_{k=1}^{N}$. Hence, the discriminator's task is to determine if the given human kinematic comes from a real videos or is a fake kinematic generated by the model.

Note that our discriminator maps to $\mathbb{R}$, because we use the Wasserstein GAN adversarial loss with gradient penalty (WGAN-GP) [39] for training. Mathematically, D^{int} and G^{int} are learnt by solving the following optimization problem,

$$
\begin{aligned}
\min_{G^{int}} \max_{D^{int}} \quad & \mathop{\mathbb{E}}_{\mathcal{Q} \sim p_r} \left[D^{int}(\mathcal{Q}) \right] \\
& - \mathop{\mathbb{E}}_{\mathbf{z} \sim \mathcal{N}(0,\mathrm{I})} \left[D^{int} \left(f_d^{int} \left(G^{int}(\mathbf{z}) \right) \right) \right] \\
& - \lambda \mathop{\mathbb{E}}_{\widehat{\mathcal{Q}} \sim p_{\widehat{\mathcal{Q}}}} \left[\left(\left\| \nabla D^{int}(\widehat{\mathcal{Q}}) \right\|_2 - 1 \right)^2 \right],
\end{aligned}
\tag{4.2}
$$

where $\lambda > 0$ is the regularizing constant, p_r is the data distribution of $\mathcal{Q}$, and $p_{\hat{\mathcal{Q}}}$ is the sampling distribution between pairs of real and fake samples. The regularizer is used to improve training as described in [39].

4.2.5 Training with a small sample size

One of the modern challenges in computer vision is to design systems that can learn from small datasets [109]. This is also our goal. Additionally, we want to learn from sample sequences of quaternions that describe intentional and non-intentional actions as accurately as possible. For this reason, we use the small, in-lab motion capture (mocap) data of [1] for training our intentional and non-intentional models (see Appendix C for a detail description of this training set).

Most human actions are of course intentional. Thus, samples of non-intentional actions are scarcer. This could lead to worse model representation for non-intentional versus intentional actions.

Fortunately, the intentional and non-intentional human actions are not independent. Constraints like plausible joint configuration applies to both, intentional and non-intentional actions. Thus, when learning the embedding space of non-intentional actions, we leverage the knowledge already learnt from intentional actions by initializing the non-intent model with the parameters of the intentional model and, then, fine-tuning using the non-intentional training set.

This process yields the trained models of intentional and non-intentional actions, CTM^{int} and $\text{CTM}^{non-int}$, respectively.

4.3 Visual Recognition and Counterfactuals

We now derive an algorithms to identify whether a never-before-seen video of a real human action is intentional or not, and another algorithm to generate never-before-seen fake videos. We use these two algorithms to derive an approach to ask and answer counterfactuals.

4.3.1 Visual recognition of intent

Given a video of a human action $\mathbf{V}$, like the one shown in Figure 4.1(a), the goal is to indicate which frames show an intentional action and which a non-intentional action.

We do recognition in in-the-wild, RGB-color videos such as the one in Figure 4.1(a). That is our *testing* data.

For each video $\mathbf{V}$, we first need to automatically extract the 3D body pose and quaternions from it. We use the algorithm of [16] to obtain the 2D landmark points of the joints and the algorithm of [63] to recover the 3D body pose of these joints. This yields a the set $\mathcal{P} = \{\mathbf{P}_i\}_{i=1}^{T}$, where $\mathbf{P}_i \in \mathbb{R}^{3d}$ is the vector of the 3D position of every joint in frame i, and d is the number of joints.

Next, we need to define the movement of the joints in the 3D body pose as quaternions. To compute the sequence of quaternions $\mathcal{Q}$ of $\mathcal{P}$, we employ a differentiable forward kinematic function $h(\cdot)$, i.e., $\mathcal{P} = h(\mathcal{Q})$. Here, we use the same forward kinematic function $h(\cdot)$ as in [72].

Thus, $\mathcal{Q} = h^{-1}(\mathcal{P})$. Unfortunately, $h(\cdot)$ is non-linear, with an infinite number of possible preimages. Thus, we need to derive an optimization approach to solve for it.

We can solve this preimage problem by finding the value of the latent variable z that minimizes the following fitting function,

$$\hat{\mathbf{z}} = \underset{\mathbf{z}}{\arg\min} \, \frac{1}{T} \sum_{i=1}^{T} \left\| \widehat{\mathbf{P}}_i - \mathbf{P}_i \right\|_2^2, \tag{4.3}$$

where $\widehat{\mathbf{P}}_i$ and $\mathbf{P}_i$ are the ith element of the sets $\widehat{\mathcal{P}}$ and $\mathcal{P}$, respectively, $\widehat{\mathcal{P}} = h(\widehat{\mathcal{Q}})$, and $\widehat{\mathcal{Q}}$ are the quaternions given by the latent variable z. Hence, $\widehat{\mathbf{P}}_i = [h(f_d(G(\mathbf{z})))]_i$, and $\mathbf{P}_i = [h(\mathcal{Q})]_i$. And, note that in the above notation we have not used the superscripts int and $non - int$, because these equations apply to both cases equally.

We use gradient descent to solve for (4.3). This yields two latent variable results, $\hat{\mathbf{z}}^{int}$ and $\hat{\mathbf{z}}^{non-int}$. The first result is given by optimizing CTM^{int}; the second by optimizing CTM$^{non-int}$. Then, $\mathcal{Q}^{int} = f_d^{int}(\hat{\mathbf{z}}^{int})$ and $\mathcal{Q}^{non-int} = f_d^{non-int}(\hat{\mathbf{z}}^{non-int})$.

As we see above, our solution yields two possible quaternions for the given 3D joint kinematics $\mathcal{P}$ of a real (RGB) video $\mathbf{V}$. The first solution, $\mathcal{Q}^{int}$, are the quaterions of $\mathcal{P}$, if the action represented by $\mathcal{P}$ were intentional. The second solution, $\mathcal{Q}^{non-int}$, are the quaterions of $\mathcal{P}$, if the action were non-intentional.

We now need to determine which of these two solutions is the correct one. We can do this by testing which of the two possible quaternions best maps to the actual kinematics of the person in the video; formally,

$$\underset{a=\{int,non-int\}}{\arg\min} \, \mathcal{L}_{err} \left(h(f_d^a(G^a(\hat{\mathbf{z}}^a))), \mathcal{P} \right), \tag{4.4}$$

where $\mathcal{L}_{err}$ is the reconstruction (or square) loss. Using the notation introduced above, we can rewrite this equation as,

$$\underset{a=\{int,non-int\}}{\arg\min} \, \frac{1}{T} \sum_{i=1}^{T} \| [h(f_d^a(G^a(\hat{\mathbf{z}}^a)))]_i - \mathbf{P}_i \|_2^2. \tag{4.5}$$

If the best reconstruction of the original kinematics is given by $\mathcal{Q}^{int}$, then we classify the action in the frames of this sequence as intentional. Otherwise, we classify the action as non-intentional.

A schematic of the above-derived approach was previously given in Figure 4.2(b).

The above equations only work for videos of length T. When the testing video contains a longer trajectory, one can choose to select multiple T-frame segments from the entire trajectory, run the classifier on each segment, and aggregate the result.

4.3.2 Generating fake videos

Having learned the underlying distribution of intentional and non-intentional actions in our embedding facilitates the generation of new sample videos never seen before. These *fake* videos are generated by our model by simply drawing samples from the learned distributions.

Formally, let $z \sim \mathcal{N}(0, I)$ be a vector in the latent space of our generators of intentional and non-intentional actions. Thus, $G^{int}(z)$ and $G^{non-int}(z)$ yields two vectors in our embedding defining an intentional and a non-intentional action, respectively. The quaternions of these actions are given by,

$$
\begin{aligned}
\mathbf{Q}^{int} &= f_d^{int}(G^{int}(z)), \\
\mathbf{Q}^{non-int} &= f_d^{non-int}(G^{non-int}(z)).
\end{aligned}
\tag{4.6}
$$

Finally, the two fake videos showing these intentional and non-intentional actions can be obtained by using a computer graphics generator to render a human body moving according to the above computed quaternions, $\mathbf{Q}^{int}$ and $\mathbf{Q}^{non-int}$. Video examples of this rendering are shown in Figure 4.4.

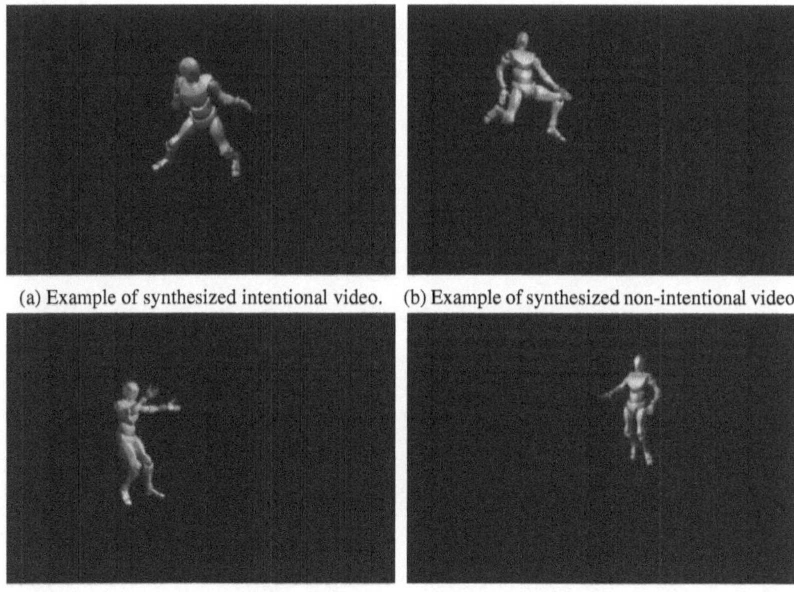

(a) Example of synthesized intentional video.　(b) Example of synthesized non-intentional video.

(c) Example of synthesized intentional video.　(d) Example of synthesized non-intentional video.

Figure 4.4: [Video] Examples of intentional and non-intentional human actions generated by our algorithm. Please click the image to play the video (Adobe Acrobat Reader required).

4.3.3　Counterfactuals

Many scientist, including Turing award winning Prof. Pearl, argue that the ability humans have to ask and answer counterfactuals is one of the major divides between human and machine intelligence [73]. Asking counterfactual means we can articulate "what ifs" questions.

In this section, we show how our algorithm can ask and answer counterfactuals in the narrow domain of the interpretation of intentional versus non-intentional actions. For example, if we detect that the action of a person transitions from intentional to non-intentional around frame t, our system can answer the counterfactual "what if the action were to stay intentional? What would it look like?", Figure 4.1(b-c). Or, the system can also ask "What other types of non-intentional actions are most likely?" and answer this too. Of course, we can also ask what would have happened at any other time t, even if the intentionality of the action did not change in the original video.

Formally, let the real video sequence be $V = \{v_1, \ldots, v_t, \ldots, v_T\}$, $1 < t < T$. We render counterfactual (fake) videos by finding the intentional and non-intentional sequences that have the most similar frames in the interval $[t - e, t]$, for some $e \in \mathbb{N}$. That is,

$$\hat{z}^{int} = \arg\min_{\mathbf{z}} \sum_{i=t-e}^{t} \left\| \left[h(f_d^{int}(G^{int}(\mathbf{z}))) \right]_i - \mathbf{P}_i \right\|_2^2, \tag{4.7}$$

and

$$\hat{\mathbf{z}}^{non-int} = \arg\min_{\mathbf{z}}$$

$$\sum_{i=t-e}^{t} \left\| \left[h(f_d^{non-int}(G^{non-int}(\mathbf{z}))) \right]_i - \mathbf{P}_i \right\|_2^2, \tag{4.8}$$

where $\mathbf{P}_i$ are the 3D joint coordinates in frame $\mathbf{v}_i$.

The quaternions of the counterfactual examples are directly given by,

$$\mathbf{Q}_{counter}^{int} = f_d^{int}(G^{int}(\hat{z}^{int})), \tag{4.9}$$

$$\mathbf{Q}_{counter}^{non-int} = f_d^{non-int}(G^{non-int}(\hat{\mathbf{z}}^{non-int})). \tag{4.10}$$

And, the mentalized (fake) videos are generated as in the previous section, using a computer graphics renderer.

4.3.4 Network design

As shown in Figure 4.3(a), the RNN encoder f_e^a, $a = \{\text{intentional, non-intentional}\}$, contains two modules, a pose encoder E_{pose} and a recurrent module. We uses a multi-layer perceptron (MLP) for E_{pose} and Gated Recurrent Unit (GRU) [21] as our recurrent module. At each time step t, the ground truth quaternion $\mathbf{Q}_t$ is first mapped to a human pose embedding using the MLP pose encoder. The GRU then takes both, the pose embedding and the previous hidden state $\mathbf{h}_{t-1}$, as inputs, and output the new hidden state $\mathbf{h}_t$. The output of the RNN encoder is the hidden state at the last frame T, h_T, which will be used as the intentional/non-intentional action embedding for the given human behavior.

The RNN decoder f_d^a contains three components as shown in Figure 4.3: a pose encoder E_{pose} (which shares its weights with the same module in the RNN encoder), a recurrent module (also a GRU), and a pose decoder D_{pose} (also an MLP). At each time step, the RNN decoder takes the previous estimated human pose $\hat{\mathbf{Q}}_{t-1}^a$ as input, passing it through the pose encoder to generate the pose embedding. Then, the pose embedding and the previous hidden state are fed to the GRU to compute the new hidden state. The pose decoder takes the current hidden state and maps it to the current estimated human pose $\hat{\mathbf{Q}}_t^a$. The initial input hidden state for the decoder is the hidden state outputted by the RNN encoder, and the initial human pose is set to a vector of zeros.

The E_{pose}, D_{pose}, and two GRU modules are trained end-to-end by minimizing the loss function given in (4.1).

Once trained, f_e^a is used to map all the intentional and non-intentional human poses onto the embedding space, where we train the GAN of section 4.2.4. We use min-max normalization for all the samples in $\mathbf{S}^a$, in each feature dimension, such that all the features are in the range of $[0, 1]$.

4.3.5 Implementation details

The RNN module in both encoder and decoder contains 2 layers of stacked GRUs, with 100 dimensional input for the human pose embedding space and 200 dimensional hidden states. The pose encoder and pose decoder are both 3-layer MLPs with the former using Rectified Linear Unit (ReLU) in all layers and the latter using ReLU in all but the last layer which uses *tanh*. Only the hidden state output from the last layer of the encoder is used to represent the human action embedding. This is also the first layer of the decoder, with its second layer initialized with a vector of all zeros (as hidden state).

For the GAN trained on the embedding space, the generator and discriminator are both 3-layer MLPs. Both generator and discriminator use ReLU in all layers but the last layer of discriminator which uses the sigmoid function.

4.3.6 Experimental details

In our experimental results reported below, we draw $\mathbf{z}$ from a standard Normal distribution defined in $\mathbb{R}^{100}$, and use $\lambda = 1$ in (4.2).

We use Adam [49] to optimize the parameters in all networks, f_e^a, f_e^a, G^a, and D^a, where $a = \{\text{intentional, non-intentional}\}$. For training f_e^* and f_e^*, the initial learning rate $= .0005$, $\beta_1 = .9$, $\beta_2 = .99$, batch size $= 128$, and we optimize for a total of 200K iteration. For training G^* and D^*, the initial learning rate $= .0001$, $\beta_1 = .9$, $\beta_2 = .99$, batch size $= 1,024$, and we use a total of 200K iteration.

In each iteration of training, we apply gradient descent to the discriminator ten times and to the generator one time. We found this approach improves stability and speeds up convergence to a desirable solution. The entire training process takes about 7 hours on a workstation with Intel Core i7-7800X and a NVIDIA TITAN Xp.

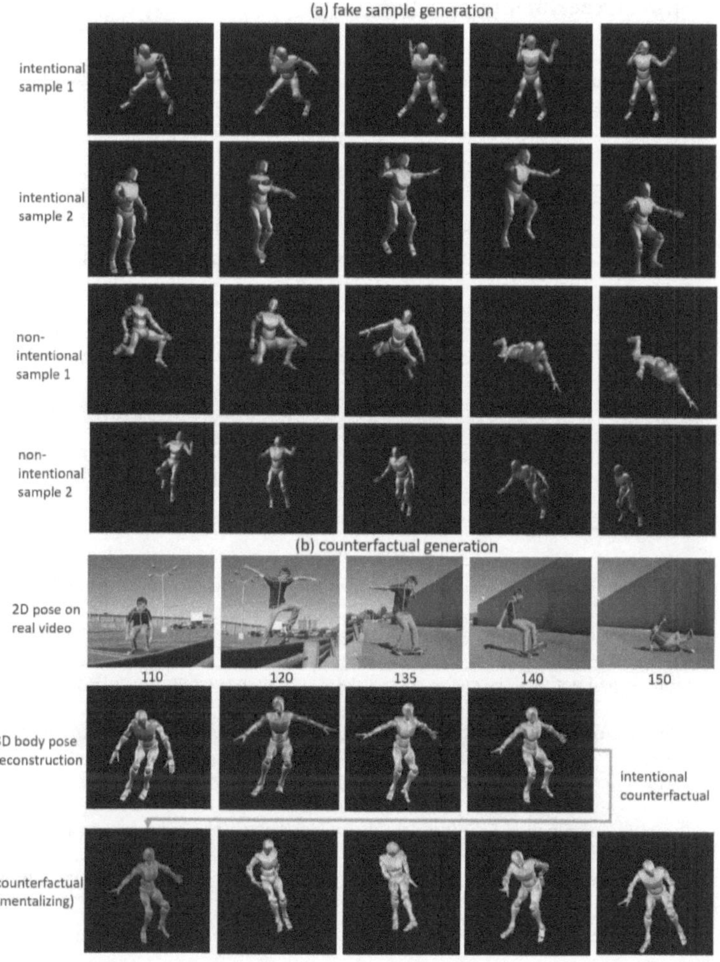

Figure 4.5: *Additional examples in Appendix C.* (a) Sample videos generated by CTM^{int} and $\text{CTM}^{non-int}$. (b) Answering a counterfactual.

4.4 Experimental Results

We start with a definition of the training and testing datasets, then provide extensive
evaluations of the proposed algorithms. *Additional experimental results are in Appendix C.*

4.4.1 Training dataset

We use the Mixamo motion capture dataset[1] to train the proposed CTM model. This
motion capture (mocap) data provides highly accurate 3D human joint position and angle
information from the direct measurement of the body markers on the agent. This is needed
to find an accurate estimate of the underlying distributions of intent and non-intent in the
embedding space. A detailed description of this dataset is available in Appendix C.

4.4.2 Testing dataset

Testing must be done in real (RGB-color) videos of actions filmed outside the lab in
non-controlled conditions, i.e., we need an in-the-wild database of intentional and non-
intentional actions. Because such a dataset does not exist, we collected our own. A short
description of this datatase is provided below. An in-depath description can be found in
Appendix C.

We downloaded $5,760$ videos from YouTube. The videos were then manually annotated to indicate whether they show an intentional or a non-intentional action by a human
annotator. Of the $5,760$ videos, $4,212$ were found to show intentional actions, and $1,548$
non-intentional actions.

[1]https://www.mixamo.com/

Next we used off-the-shelf algorithms to extract the 3D location of the joints of the body of the people in the videos. We found that OpenPose [16] yielded accurate 2D landmark detections in our dataset, and the algorithm of [62] yielded accurate 3D coordinate estimates.

4.4.3 Visual recognition of intent

For each testing video we first extract the sequence of 3D joint position as introduced in Section 4.4.2. The sequence is then split into 60-frame segments with no overlap, $T = 60$. If at least one of these segments is classified as non-intentional, then the video is said to be showing an non-intentional action.

We compare the results of this algorithm to the manual annotations described in the preceding section, yielding a classification accuracy of **82.35%**. Comparative results with standard deep nets are in Table B.1. To get these comparative results, each network was trained using the set $\mathcal{P}$ of each training sample. Testing is done on the set $\mathcal{P}$ extracted from each real video in our testing set.

Also, note that during testing, our algorithm needs to optimize (4.3). We do so with Adam [49], learning rate $= .005$, $\beta_1 = .9$, and $\beta_2 = .999$. The optimization stops when the loss does not improve for 100 iterations or the number of iteration reaches $1,000$, whichever comes first.

4.4.4 Generating fake videos and counterfactuals

We use the algorithms described above to generate fake video (i.e., mentalize unseen actions). We ran two different types of experiments.

Figure 4.5(a-b) shows example fake videos of intentional and non-intentional actions generated by our algorithm. To generate these fake video examples, we randomly draw

Method	Accuracy
RNN	49.77%
ResNet	51.03%
Ours	**82.35%**

Table 4.1: Comparative results for the visual recognition of intent, with a RNN classifier with GRU modulem and a 50-layer deep residual network, ResNet.

a sample vector $\mathbf{z} \sim \mathcal{N}(\mathbf{0}, \mathbf{I})$, where $\mathbf{I}$ is the identity matrix in $\mathbb{R}^{100}$. This vector is thus given in our latent space. The fake sample associated to this vector is given by equation (4.6). The generated quaternion sequence is then exported as BVH file with the skeleton template matched with T-pose in Mixamo dataset. The BVH file and character body are then combined in AutoDesk Maya 2015 to render the final video.

In our second set of experiments, we provide visual answers to counterfactual questions. Two examples are given in Figures 4.1 and 4.5(c); additional exmaples are in Appendix C. These counterfactuals are given by equation (4.9).

4.5   Conclusions

We have presented, to our knowledge, the first algorithm able to render (fake) videos of intentional and non-intentional actions and shown how to use this algorithm to recognize whether an newly observed action is performed intentionally or not, and to answer counterfactual questions, Table B.1 and Figure 4.5.

Chapter 5: Adding Knowledge to Unsupervised Algorithms for the Recognition of Intent

5.1 Introduction

To solve high-level computer vision problems, like object recognition and action understanding, researchers and practitioners typically use very large datasets of manually labeled data to train a machine learning algorithm. These algorithms are typically used to discriminate between different categories, e.g., cars versus bikes, or running versus walking [20, 114]. Ideally, one would want to be able to design systems that can perform high-level task like these without the need of any manually annotated data.

One way to derive such unsupervised computer vision algorithms is to incorporate knowledge into the system. Here, we derive one such approach and use it to recognize intentional and non-intentional actions. We use Aristotle's definition of intent as something deliberate, chosen before the start of the action [8]. This definition is also included in Cartesian dualism, where Descartes differentiated conscious, intentional actions from reflexes caused by external stimuli [27].

To successfully classify a perceived action as intentional or unintentional, we need to carefully evaluate each segment of the video sequence displaying it. To clarify, consider the following example. A person is walking down a hall and after a few seconds slips and falls to the ground (maybe the floor is wet). Here, we would say that the person was intentionally walking down the hall, but that he unintentionally slipped and fell. Afterwards, he intentionally stood up and continued walking. Compare this to the case where the person does not slip but is instead pushed to the ground by someone else. In this case, we say that all segments in the scene are performed intentionally (since the fall is the result of the intentional push). Our goal is to derive an algorithm that can correctly and fully automatically annotate each segment of a video sequence as showing an intentional or a non-intentional action.

As mentioned above, to solve this problem, one could manually annotate a large number of video segments showing intentional and non-intentional actions and then use a machine learning algorithm to learn to discriminate between the two. Unfortunately, the collection and annotation of a sufficiently large dataset has a considerable cost. A major research direction in computer vision is to derive algorithm that can solve problems like ours in a completely unsupervised way, i.e., without the use of any labelled training data.

We solve this problem by adding knowledge to our system. Specifically, we use the basic knowledge of self-propelled motion, Newtonian motion and their relationship to reason about intentionality of an action. We derive a simple unsupervised computer vision algorithm for the recognition of intent based on these concepts. This demonstrates how simple, common concepts can be used to design systems that can perform complex, high-level tasks even when large amounts of labelled training data are not available.

5.2　Related works

Visual recognition of intent in human. The mechanism of visual recognition of intent has been the interest of congitive and social science since 1960s, although its underlying behavioral and neural mechanism is still an open question. The seminal work from Heider and Simmel [42] shows that human subjects can assign personal attribute (like intentionality) to abstract geometric shape when the object moves in a human-like manner. [85] shows that body movement plays an important role in human intent recognition. [57] studied the capability of infants attributing goals to human and non-human agents when the agent moves in a self-propelled manner, supporting the hypothesis that the part of the recognition capability is rooted in a specialized reasoning system activated based on the kinematic feature of the object's action. [18, 19] showed that intent recognition involves in an interplay of the kinematic information of the agent and prior expectation of the agent's movement.

Visual recognition of intention in computer vision. Although significant progress has been made in some vision tasks like face/object recognition, there is very few studies focusing on visual recognition of intent of agent. [110] proposed a hierarchical graph that jointly models attention and intention from a RGB-D video of an agent. But the study was focusing on the intention behind the eye gaze (the definition of attention in the study). [105] proposed an algorithm to infer the motivation of the agent from an image with common knowledge factor graph extracted from text. [80] introduces an algorithm of estimate agent intention from the 3D skeleton of the upper body of the agent. In the study the intention is represented by latent state space defining the location of agent's arms, whose dynamic is defined by a neural network. This latent variable is then estimated by Expectation-Maximization (EM) algorithm. [103] developed an algorithm to infer a binary goal (help or hinder) of in a multi-agent setup with inverse planing in Markov Decision Process (MDP). Most of these works are based on a data-driven supervised model, which requires a large amount of labeled training data.

Another area of research that is also related to the visual recognition of intent is human action/motion forecasting [84]. Motion prediction aims at predicting actions from one or multiple agents in the future based on the observed actions in the past, where the intention recognition plays an important role (albeit very differently from the proposed study). [31] uses the 2D human pose to estimate pedestrians' intention of crossing and cyclists' intention of turning and stopping. [104], which also addresses the problem of pedestrian crossing/non-crossing recognition, shows that among different combinations of handcrafted/deep features with data-driven learning models, CNN deep feature and SVM shows the best performance on Joint Attention for Autonomous Driving (JAAD) dataset.

Although the aforementioned works shared the name of "intent recognition" with our study, the task is however very different. First, the purpose of this study is to recognize intentionality, i.e., recognizing whether an observed action is performed intentionally or not, rather than predicting the future human behavior based on a confined set of actions. In other words, our study is focusing on understanding the past, rather than predicting the future. Second, the previous works focusing on recognizing different intentions, with the assumption that all actions from an agent are intentional. However, this assumption might not hold for an arbitrary action (the action might be non-intentional), which can be tested by our algorithm. To our knowledge, there is no published computer vision system for the recognition of intentional/non-intentional action.

Common knowledge in computer vision. Incorporating common sense knowledge in computer vision system is also a largely unexplored territory in the community. [4, 26]

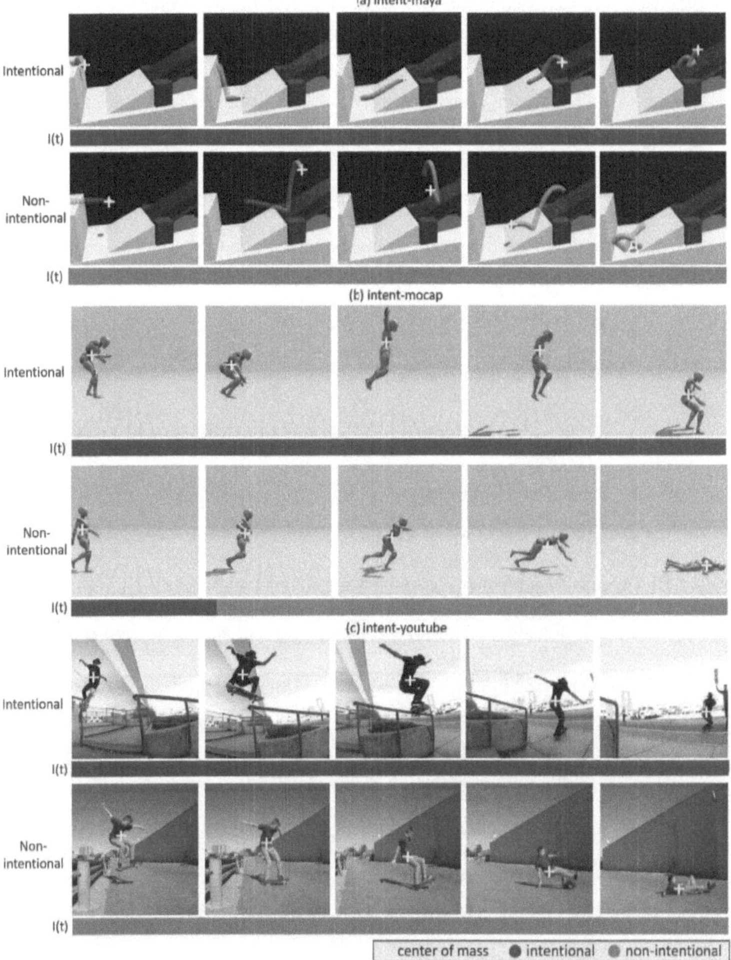

Figure 5.1: Recognizing intentional versus non-intentional actions. The six samples are from the three datasets introduced in Section 5.5.1. The colored horizontal bar underneath each image sequence denotes an intentionality function $I(t)$ of the action. The yellow crosshair illustrates the 2D project of the location of agent's center of mass. (a) intent-maya dataset. The transparent tail of the ball shows the location of the agent in the last second. (b) intent-mocap dataset. (c) intent-youtube dataset.

proposed rule based commonsense reasoning systems for visual scene understanding and action recognition, but with a focus on only hand related actions. [117] introduced the task of so called "visual commonsense reasoning" with corresponding dataset, where the machine is asked not only to answer question about the action and interaction between agent, but also the rationale behind such action. The rationale of an action is not directly observable in the given image, thus must be inferred through commonsense reasoning.

5.3   Visual Recognition of Intent

5.3.1   Problem Formulation

Our goal is to design an unsupervised computer vision system that can classify observed actions of an agent or object as intentional or not. Given the trajectory of the agent's (object's) center of mass, we would like to parse the trajectory into segments that either exhibit intentional movement or unintentional movement.

Let the 3D location of the agent (object) as a function of t be denoted by $\mathbf{p}(t) = (x(t), y(t), z(t))^T$, with $y(t)$ indicating the vertical axis pointing up (i.e., up defines the positive quadrant).

We now define the intentionality of the action of the agent as $I(t) \in \{1, -1\}$, with 1 indicating the action is intentional and -1 non-intentional; note $I(\cdot)$ is also a function of time, since some parts of the observed action may correspond to intentional actions (e.g., walking), while others to non-intentional (e.g., lose one's footing).

Hence, our goal is to construct a model $f(\cdot)$ such that $I(t) = f(\mathbf{p}(t))$. Since we wish to do so without any training or the need for labeled data (i.e., an unsupervised approach), herein, we derive a model of $f(\cdot)$ which incorporates common knowledge about intentional and non-intentional behavior of an agent.

Figure 5.1 provides six examples of this task, ranging from animations of abstract geometric objects (intent-maya, Figure 5.1(a)), to animations of humanoid characters (intent-mocap, Figure 5.1(b)), then to real-world video of human actions (intent-youtube, Figure 5.1(c)). The colored horizontal bar in Figure 5.1 denotes an $I(t)$ of an action. Our task is to construct a model that maps the 3D trajectory of the agent's center of mass (shown as yellow crosshairs in Figure 5.1) to the intentionality of the agent's action $I(t)$ (blue/red horizontal bar in Figure 5.1).

5.3.2 Common knowledge concepts

Imagine a human agent jumping over a hurdle, which is clearly an intentional action. When she prepares to jump, she converts the (non-observable) chemical energy stored in her body to the mechanical energy of her muscle. The muscle contracts and pushes her body upward in the air. While in the air, gravity is the main external force acting on her which forces her to fall back to the ground. If the initial muscle contraction is strong enough, she successfully jumps over the hurdle.

If we examine the total mechanical energy of the system in the above example, which includes the scene and the agent, we see stable energy before the jump, a sharp increase at the time of the jump, and a stable trend after the jump (during free fall back down). For us human, the association between the perception of intentionality and the function of total mechanical energy is among many common knowledge concepts that we gradually learn in the early stage of the development of our brain [57]. Our goal is to incorporate this knowledge into a computer vision system, thus avoiding the need to train a supervised machine learning algorithm to model intentionality from labelled data.

This study models the following common knowledge concepts,

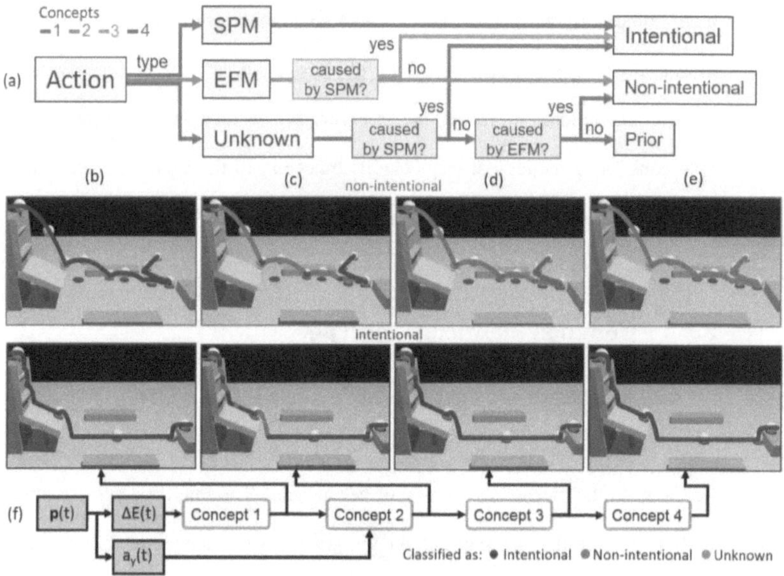

Figure 5.2: Overview of the proposed algorithm. Here we illustrate the concepts we derive to model intentionality. (a) shows a logic diagram of the four concepts introduced in Section 5.3.2, and their relationship with intentionality. (b-e) shows a pair of samples from our dataset described in Section 5.5.1. The intentional example (in the blue box) shows a ball stepping down a ladder and jumping down an inclined platform to go to the isle at the far end of the scene. In the non-intentional example, the ball rolls and bounces according to Newtonian physics, with a trajectory that closely mimics that of the intentional action, yet the human eye is not trick by this and people clearly classify the first action as intentional and the second as non-intentional. (b) Result of our algorithm when only Concept 1 is considered; (c) result with Concepts 1 and 2; (d) result with Concepts 1, 2 and 3; (e) results with all four concepts included in our algorithm; (f) model overview. The proposed algorithm first extract change in total mechanical energy $\Delta E(t)$ and the vertical acceleration $a_y(t)$ from the input trajectory of the agent, $\mathbf{p}(t)$. Concept 1 recognizes intentional action from $\Delta E(t)$. Concept 2 takes $a_y(t)$ and the output of Concept 1 to form an understanding on non-intentional actions, which will be used in Concept 3 to update the decision. Finally, Concept 4 handles all the unknown state that is previously unrecognizable (see derivation in the main text of the paper for details).

- **Concept 1 (C1):** A standalone[2] self-propelled motion (SPM) is an intentional action, where self-propelled motion (SPM) is any movement that adds observable mechanical energy into the system.

- **Concept 2 (C2):** A standalone external-force motion (EFM) is a non-intentional action, where the external-force motion (EFM) is any movement induced only by external forces (e.g., gravity).

- **Concept 3 (C3):** An EFM caused by a SPM is part of an intentional action (e.g., falling down after an upward jump).

- **Concept 4 (C4):** An agent has inertia of intentionality (II), meaning the intentionality of an agent does not change unless C1-C3 applies.

The four concepts and their relationship with the intentionality of an action can be visualized by Figure 5.2(a) in the form of a logic diagram.

Similar to Newton's Three Laws of Motion, any of these concepts alone does not fully define intentional/non-intentional actions across time. Only when combined, they form a common knowledge system that can be used to recognize intentionality for an agent across time.

5.3.3 Mathematical derivations

Recall that we want to formulate the common knowledge as a functional mapping $f(\cdot)$, such that $I(t) = f(\mathbf{p}(t))$, where $I(t)$ and range of $\{-1, 1\}$ at each time t. During the definition of each Concept 1 and 2, we will also use 0 to denote an "unknown" state, which is an intermediate state that will be categorized in Concept 4.

---

[2]Standalone means this concept only focuses on the movement at a specific time point rather than the relationship between actions.

Concept 1

Concept 1 (C1) states that a standalone SPM is an intentional actions since SPM adds total mechanical energy to the observable system. C1 derives from the common knowledge that human utilizes internally stored energy to execute movements that fulfill his/her intention, adding observable energy into the system. Thus the model of C1 can be derived as follows,

$$I_{C1}(t) = f_{C1}(\mathbf{p}(t)) = \begin{cases} 1 & \text{if } \Delta E(t) > 0 \\ 0 & \text{otherwise,} \end{cases} \tag{5.1}$$

where $\Delta E(t) = dE(t)/dt$ is the change in the total observable mechanical energy $E(t)$ with respect to time,

$$E(t) = K(t) + V(t), \tag{5.2}$$

with $K(t)$ the kinetic energy given by,

$$K(t) = \frac{1}{2}\left[\left(\frac{dx(t)}{dt}\right)^2 + \left(\frac{dy(t)}{dt}\right)^2 + \left(\frac{dz(t)}{dt}\right)^2\right], \tag{5.3}$$

$V(t)$ the potential energy defined as,

$$V(t) = G\left(y(t) - y(t_0)\right), \tag{5.4}$$

G is the gravitational constant, and $y(t_0)$ is the initial y-axis location of the agent. In this formulation, we model agents as points with unit masses, neglecting the rotational kinetic energy or elastic potential energy.

$I_{C1}(t)$ will be equal to 1 at any instance in which the trajectory adds energy into the observable system and 0 to any other movement that does not specified in this concept.

Concept 2

Concept 2 (C2) states that a standalone EFM, a motion introduced by only external forces, is non-intentional. This is due to the fact that the exertion of the external force does not change depending on agent's desire or belief. For example, if an agent is falling, it is generally not the intention of the agent to be falling but, rather, the agent has no control over the effect of gravity, making this downward motion inevitable and, thus, non-intentional [111]. However, one should also notice that an agent may take advantage of the EFM, intentionally position themselves in the EFM to achieve their purpose. This special condition will be considered in concept 3.

In practice, the number and types of external forces vary depending on the scene. But on earth, gravity is the primary external force we are bound by and, hence, this is what we are focusing on in the present work.

There are two characteristics of gravity: 1. It is approximately equal regardless of the location of the agent, thus introducing a constant downward acceleration (g); 2. the effect of gravity on an agent (or object) does not increase the observable total mechanical energy of the system. The former will be modeled by $f_{C2g}(\mathbf{p}(t))$, while the latter is already modeled by Concept 1 and represented in $I_{C1}(t)$.

With this knowledge, we can derive the model of C2, f_{C2}, as,

$$
\begin{aligned}
I_{C2}(t) &= f_{C2}(\mathbf{p}(t), I_{C1}(t)) \\
&= f_{C2g}(\mathbf{p}(t)) + I_{C1}(t),
\end{aligned}
\tag{5.5}
$$

where $f_{C2g}(\mathbf{p}(t))$ is defined as,

$$
f_{C2g}(\mathbf{p}(t)) = \begin{cases} -1 & \text{if } I_{C1}(t) = 0 \wedge a_y(t) = c \cdot g, \\ & \exists\, c > 0 \\ 0 & \text{otherwise,} \end{cases}
\tag{5.6}
$$

g is the negative acceleration due to gravity, $\wedge$ is the Boolean AND operation, and $a_y(t)$ is the vertical acceleration of the agent, which is defined as,

$$
a_y(t) = \frac{d^2 y(t)}{dt^2}.
\tag{5.7}
$$

Note that we defined the y-axis to be pointing vertically upward, opposite to the direction of gravity.

The condition for -1 (non-intentional) in the equation (5.6), $a_y(t) = c \cdot g, \ \exists\, c > 0$ represents a downward, constant acceleration. The other condition $I_{C1}(t) = 0$ showing the movement does not add anything to the total mechanical energy of the observable system. The two conditions are combined with an AND operator to ensure that both are simultaneously satisfied.

One may wonder why $c > 0$, rather than $c = 1$, meaning the vertical acceleration of the agent is equal to the gravitational acceleration on earth. The reason is that by having $c > 0$ we can model the motion due to gravity when the agent is on an inclined surface. The case that the object moved in a uniform speed ($c = 0$) is assigned to the unknown state under this concept since the motion is not due to mere gravity.

Equation (5.5) adds f_{C2g} and I_{C1} together, which gives 1 for intentional, -1 for non-intentional, and 0 for all the unknown movement that are not described by either C1 or C2. Those unknown movements will be handled by Concept 4.

Concept 3

Concept 3 (C3), as foreshadowed in Section 5.3.3, describes the condition that an EFM might not be non-intentional when the agent actively moves herself to the status of EFM. For example, when the human agent was jumping over the hurdle mentioned earlier in this section, she was subjected to gravity forces after she pushes herself in the air. Although the free fall motion is induced by mere gravity, the motion is nevertheless the result of her initial jump – an intentional action that adds total mechanical energy into the system. C3

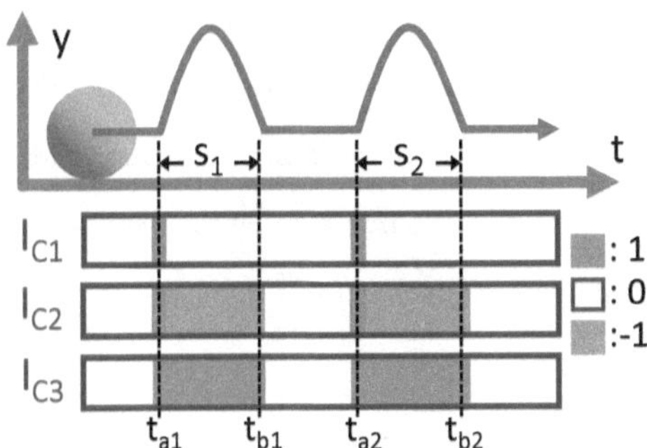

Figure 5.3: An example where Concept 3 is necessary to achieve a correct classification of intentionallity. In this trajectory, an agent jumps twice. I_{C1}, I_{C2} and I_{C3} is the output of Concepts 1, 2 and 3, respectively. At time t_{a1} and t_{a2}, the agent adds positive energy into the system to initialize the jumps. Thus, the movement at these two time points is detected as intentional as shown in I_{C1}. s_1 and s_2 are the two time intervals when the agent's movement is induced only by gravity, i.e., free fall. Hence, the action in these two intervals is detected as non-intentional by I_{C2}. However, since the free fall is part of the jump, the correct classification should be intentional. By taking into account causal relationship between action, Concept 3 can correctly classify these two movement as intentional, as shown in I_{C3}.

is modeling exactly this condition, when a EFM is casused by a SFM, this EFM should be classified as intentional movement.

However, modeling the causal relationship between actions is a challenging problem by itself. In this study, we simplify the causality to an immediate temporal relationship, i.e., the causal action is immediately before the consequential action, which is a surrogate we found works well. Temporal precedence is one of the criteria that is necessary for constructing causality. The reason we only focus on short-term causality is that the long-term causal relationship between actions can be decomposed to a chain of short-term causal relationships between actions.

To model this knowledge, let us first define the set of time intervals of all EFMs as $S_{\text{EFM}} = \{s_1, s_2, ..., s_i, ...\}$ whose elements s_i are the time interval of the ith EFM, as shown in Fig 5.3. The main idea of the algorithm is, for each EFM, identify if it is caused by a SFM. If so, EFM will be recognized as an intentional action. More formally, the model f_{C3} is formulated as shown in Algorithm 1.

Algorithm 1: Algorithm for C3

Input: I_{C1}, S_{EFM} ;
Output: I_{C3} ;
Initialize $I_{C3} \leftarrow I_{C1}$;
for $s_i \in S_{\text{EFM}}$ **do**
    $t_{ai} \leftarrow \inf(s_i)$;
    if $I_{C1}(t_{ai} - 1) == 1$ **then**
        $I_{C3}(t) \leftarrow 1$ for $\forall t \in s_i$;
    end
end

In Algorithm 1, $t_{ai} \leftarrow \inf(s_i)$ extracts the starting time point for the ith EFM. The operation of $I_{C1}(t_{ai} - 1) == 1$ examine if the movement immediate preceding EFM is a SFM. In such case, SFM is treated as the cause of EFM, which means EFM is also intentional. The assignment of intentionality is implemented as $I_{C3}(t) \leftarrow 1$, for $\forall t \in s_i$ in the algorithm.

Figure 5.3 illustrates an example of the case where C3 is needed for correct recognition of intentionality. There are two EFMs in the figure, whose time intervals are denoted by s_1 and s_2. There are two instances of SPMs, which can both be abstracted as force impulse generated by the agent that initializes a "jump". Since the instantaneous nature of the impulse, our C1 model can only detect the SPM at two time points, t_{a1} and t_{b1} shown in the I_{C1} row in the figure. The two EFMs, which are free fall in this case, is a direct and expected result from the initial SPM, thus should be treated as intentional.

Concept 4

Concept 4 (C4) is introduced to handle intentional movements that are not modeled by C1, C2 and C3. Using the concept of inertia from physics, which describes a resistance of the object to change its velocity, we describe C4 as an *intentionality inertia*, a property of the agent that resists changes in its intentionality status – the intentionality of an agent does not change unless the one or more of concepts 1 through 3 occur.

The rationale behind this concept can also be understood from the causal relationship of the actions. When a movement causes another movement, the intentionality carries over. However, if an event happens that breaks the causal relationship, in our case those event defined by the C1 to C3, the intentionality will change accordingly. Let us imagine a case in which a human agent falls from a cliff, hits the ground and lies on the ground since then. The unfortunate fall is a non intentional movement, according to C2. The movement (or lack of movement) of lying on the ground is also non-intentional. It is not the agent's intention to fall at the first place, so it is also not the intention of the agent to be lying on the ground since lying on the ground is an effect of the falling and hitting the ground. Thus, although "lying on the ground" is not one of the actions defined in C1 to C3 (does not add total mechanical energy; does not have a constant downward acceleration), it is still non-intentional due to its relationship to its cause action. If the agent standing up after lying on the floor, the "standing up" will be recognized as intentional according to C1.

To model this concept, we first define a set of time interval of all the "unknown" actions, $U_{\text{null}} = \{u_1, u_2, ..., u_i, ...\}$ whose element u_i is the time interval of the i-th unknown movement - the ones that does not belong to C1 to C3. For each of the unknown movement, we check the intentionality of the previous action, and assign the previous intentionality state to the current unknown action. More formally, the concept is formulated in algorithm 2.

Algorithm 2: Algorithm for C4

Input: I_{C3}, U_{null} ;
Output: I_{C4} ;
Initialize $I_{C4} \leftarrow I_{C3}$;
for $u_i \in U_{\text{null}}$ **do**
$\quad\quad t_{ai} \leftarrow \inf(u_i)$;
$\quad\quad I_{\text{cause}} = I_{C3}(t_{ai} - 1)$;
$\quad\quad I_{C4}(t) \leftarrow I_{\text{cause}}$ for $\forall t \in u_i$;
end

One may wonder what if the unknown movement happens at the beginning of the video where there is no C1-C3 motion defined as cause. In those cases, prior knowledge about the nature of the agent is needed, i.e., the assumption about the default intentionality of the agent. For a human agent, one might want to assume the default state is intentional, since the action from a normal, conscious adult is generally intentional by default (otherwise there is no reason for that person to move). In the case that no prior knowledge is available, the algorithm will output the unknown states.

Now that we derived all the implementation of concepts 1-4, the final $I(t)$ is directly equal to $I_{C4}(t)$. Note that although $I(t) = I_{C4}(t)$, $I(t)$ is also a combination of all four concepts, since $I_{C4}(t)$ is a function of $I_{C3}(t)$ which itself is a function of both $I_{C1}(t)$ and $I_{C2}(t)$ (shown in Algorithm 1 and Algorithm 2).

5.3.4   Implementation Details

To apply our algorithm on the trajectories with discrete time (frames), we use 1st order finite difference to approximate the derivative. We applied a 30-frame median filter on the estimated total mechanical energy from equation (5.2) to remove outliers. The condition that compared to zero in equation (5.1,5.6) will replace zero with a positive threshold close to zero to account for possible numerical error in the estimation.

5.4   Assumptions of the system

In this section, we will give a thorough analysis on the assumptions of the proposed algorithm. We will delineate the assumptions made on the Computational Level (Section 5.3.2) and the Algorithmic Level (Section 5.3.3)[3].

We argue that the proposed common knowledge concepts are relatively general on the computational level, meaning that the logic described by the four concepts are generally sufficient to determine intentionality across layers of abstraction (the same logic can be applied to Heider-Simmel-like animations as well as real word videos). However, the algorithmic implementation we used is based on a set of assumptions which limits its generality. To explain this, let us consider an example of a cue ball hitting a pool ball. In this example, when the interested agent is the pool ball, the movement is due to an external-force movement, induced by the impulse from the cue ball. Because this EFM is not a result of a self-propelled motion, the algorithm, on the conceptual level, should correctly classify the movement as non-intentional. But, on the algorithmic level, our specific algorithmic implementation is telling a different story. Because the ball gains mechanical energy (through

---

[3]Here we are using the Computational, Algorithmic, and Implementational level from David Marr [60]. The implementational level is not discussed since our work does not contribute to that specific level

the impulse from the cue ball), the algorithm determines that the pool ball is performing self-propelled motion, and thus annotate the movement as intentional.

The reason for the mismatch, is because of the following assumptions our algorithm operates on:

1. There is only one agent involved in the action.

2. The total mechanical energy of the agent can be calculated from its kinematics of the center of mass.

3. The external force is gravity and its decomposition.

4. The causal relationship between SPM and EFM can be described with immediate temporal relationship.

The four assumptions listed here might lead to the impression that the proposed system is very constrained. This might be true compared to the generic intention recognition, which is extremely complex and even humans fail to perform this task in cases. However, under the condition of action from a single agent in a static environment on earth, the set of assumptions are generally applicable, or could be approximated well enough for the algorithm to perform well, which we will show in the experimental results in Section 5. The clear presentation of assumptions, we argue, should be considered as an advantage rather than a weakness, since it allows practitioners to be aware of the condition where our algorithm is not applicable, and provides researchers clear future directions of improvement.

5.5 Experiments

To our knowlege, there is no existed dataset on intentional/non-intentional actions. Thus, we created three datasets for our experiment: intent-maya, intent-mocap and intent-youtube. Intent-maya dataset contains abstract minimalistic 3D animation for intentional/non-intentional actions, providing 3D ground truth trajectory for sphere-like agent. Intent-mocap dataset contains motion capture data collected from human agents, providing accurate 3D location of human body but left the center of mass trajectory subject to estimation. Intent-youtube dataset provides in-the-wild RGB video samples where 3D location of human body and center of mass are both estimated. Although we provide manual labels of intentionality on all the three datasets, those labels are not used as part of our proposed algorithm, since our algorithm is not data-driven thus has no need for manual labels. The label is only used to evaluate the performance of the proposed algorithm and train the supervised baselines for comparison. Testing on these three datasets shows the capability of our algorithm to recognize intentionality in both abstract, idealistic dataset and realistic, noisy dataset, showing the general applicability of the proposed concepts.

5.5.1 Datasets

Intent-maya dataset

Intent-maya datasets contains 60 3D animations of agents acting intentionally or non-intentionally, half for each class. The animations are designed similar to the stimuli in the classical Heider and Simmel experiment [42], in which they showed that human attribute intentionality even to abstract geometric objects. In our videos, one or multiple balls move in a manually designed 3D scene. The movement is human-like in intentional videos and Newtonian in the non-intentional videos. We use Autodesk Maya 2015 to generate the videos. Keyframe animation is used for the intentional videos and Bullet Physical Engine is used for the non-intentional videos. Each video has 480 frames at 60 fps.

To ensure the videos can be perceived as intentional or nonintentional, we asked 30 Amazon Mechanical Turkers to evaluate each animation, judging if the action is intentional or not. All the videos in the dataset has at least 90% agreement among Turkers indicating a consistent intentionality perception across human subjects.

Since all animation are manually coded, we can extract the ground truth 3D trajectory of the center of mass of the agent directly from Maya animation.

Intent-mocap dataset

The 3D manually designed animation we created in Maya provided abstract but yet compelling intentional/ non-intentional perception on balls. However, one may view the animation in intent-maya dataset as too abstract and simple to be generalized to practical condition. Intent-mocap dataset is created to mediate this concern. Motion capture data provides us actions performed by human agent with the advantage of direct measurement on 3D location of body markers, yielding accurate 3D trajectories of the joints of the agent.

We collect mocap sequences from Adobe Mixamo dataset[4], which provide a wide range of intentional and non-intentional mocap sequences that are cleaned by keyframe animators. We manually select the intentional and non-intentional sample based on the action description provided in the datasets. The description for intentional actions includes jumping, walking, running, climbing, etc. The description of non-intentional actions includes, falling, tripping, slipping, etc. With these description, we collected total 208 samples, half for each class. A sequence of 21-joint skeleton is extracted from the mocap samples using

[4]https://www.mixamo.com/

91

MATLAB. The range of length the sequence varies from 32 to 1219 frames. The sampling rate of the sequence is 60 Hz.

We directly use the 3D human joints location provided the mocap data.

Intent-youtube dataset

The mocap dataset provides precise human action sequence. However, the nature of the mocap generally requires the actors to perform pre-scripted actions. Thus even if we collect non-intentional samples, one could argue that the actor is to "pretend" to be non-intentional[5]. We introduce intent-youtube dataset to address this concern.

The youtube datasets contains 1000 in-the-wild human action videos, among which 500 are intentional actions and 500 are non-intentional actions. The videos are collected by keyword searching in YouTube. For intentional video, the keywords are derived from "action" and "activity" in WordNet [65] and ConceptNet [93]. Non-intentional keywords consist two part: adjective and action (e.g., "accidental drop"). Besides the keywords extracted from WordNet and ConceptNet, we also used keywords that empirically effective, like "fail" for non-intentional actions. Only the videos with above 100 views are used in our dataset. Camera shot detection is applied to each video to ensure each video clip only contains one camera. The video clips with significant camera motion are also removed from the dataset. All video samples have at least one full body agent. The final videos varied between 51 and 299 frames in length.

To verify that these video properly exhibit either an intentional or unintentional action, each video was classified into the intent or non-intent categories by a Amazon Mechanical

---

[5]However, one should also notice that acting to be non-intentional does not mean the action and kinematics of the agent lacks the characteristic of the genuine non-intentional movement

Turker and then verified by an experienced annotator. All the videos with inconsistent judgment from the annotators are removed from the dataset.

We extract 3D human pose by applying 3D human pose estimation algorithm proposed in [63] on the 2D human pose extracted by OpenPose [16]. Given a estimated 3D human pose, we solve a perspective n-point (PnP) problem with non-linear least square (with steepest decent algorithm) to estimate the 3D translation of the agent.

5.5.2 Estimating center of mass for human agent

To estimate the center of mass of the human agent, we first assign each joint to either legs (from hip to the toe), torso (lower back, spine, lower spine and head) and arms (shoulder, elbow, wrist and hand). Then the center of mass of each human body component was computed by averaging all the points assigned to the body part. The center of mass of the agent is then calculated by weighted averaging the body part center, with the weight defined by the standard human weight distribution [98], see Figure 5.4.

5.5.3 Recognition of intent in videos

The algorithm introduced in Section 5.3 recognizes intentionality in each segment for a single agent, which has to be aggregated for the final intentionality label for the entire video.

For the samples in intent-maya datasets, we know that each video either contains purely intentional or purely non-intentional actions. Thus if the number of detected intentional segment is greater than the nonintentional segments, the video is intentional, and *vice versa*. More formally, the final decision for the video, I_v is defined as follows,

$$I_v = \begin{cases} \text{intentional} & \text{if } \sum_{j=1}^{N} \sum_{t=1}^{T_j} I_{C4,j}(t) > 0 \\ \text{nonintentional} & \text{otherwise} \end{cases} \tag{5.8}$$

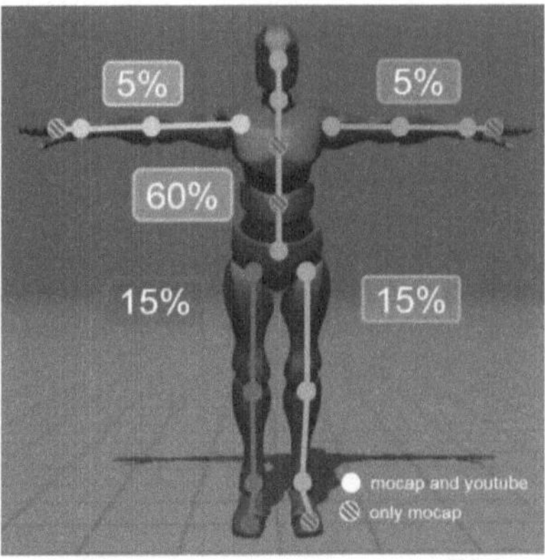

Figure 5.4: Illustration of weight distribution used in calculating center of mass in the mocap and youtube datasets. The joints with solid color are used in both mocap and youtube skeleton template. The joints with diagonal pattern are only used in the mocap skeleton template.

where $I_{C4,j}(t)$ denotes the result of C4 for the j-th agents in the video. $\sum_{t=1}^{T_j} I_{C4,j}(t)$ denotes the difference between the number of intentional segments versus non-intentional segments for j-th agent, which is calculated by summation since intentional action is labeled as 1 and non-intentional as -1.

Unlike the sphere-like agent in the intent-maya dataset, the non-intentional action of human agents is usually happen in the middle of intentional actions (e.g., a human slips in the middle of a walk, with walking as intentional but slipping as non-intentional). Thus we recognize the action of the agent as non-intentional if the number non-intentional segments is above a threshold (we set threshold equal to 40 frames in our experiment). Otherwise the action of the agent in the video is intentional.

5.5.4   Comparison between our algorithm and baseline methods

We first compare our algorithm against 4 baseline methods: Linear Discriminate Analysis (LDA), Nearest Neighbour (NN), Kernel Subclass Discriminant Analysis (KSDA) [115], a deep residual network (ResNet) [41], a recurrent neural network with Long Short Term Memory modules (LSTM), and a recurrent neural network with attention mechanism (LSTM+attention). For the latter two baselines (LSTM and LSTM+attention) we also test their performance with RGB video as input rather than 3D trajectories with an additional baseline from R(2+1)D [99]. These collection of baselines represents a wide spectrum of methods ranging from simple linear method to modern deep learning based method. The performance on these methods will show the level of difficulties of the problem of intent recognition.

Implementation detail for LDA, NN and KSDA

For LDA, NN and KSDA, we first applied a 30-frame sliding window with a step size of 15 to the trajectory of each agent. We then used Discrete Cosine Transformation (DCT) to map each x, y, z component of the trajectory segment to a 10 dimensional space of DCT coefficients, which defines a 30 dimensional feature space. Samples extracted from different agents are pooled together to form the training set. During testing, the classification is first conducted on the segment level and then the same thresholding method is used as in Section 5.5.3. 10-fold cross-validation is used to partition the datasets to training and testing.

Implementation Detail for ResNet

For ResNet, instead of handcrafting the feature space, we directly input 3D trajectory segment to the network and have the network learn the feature representation for classification. Same sliding window and cross-validation method is used as in the LDA, NN and KSDA. We used ResNet-18 with modification on the first convolutional layer and maxpooling layer to accomodate the input dimensionality of the 3D trajectory segment. The kernel size of the first convolutional layer is 7×3 with padding $= 2$. For the fisrt maxpooling layer, the kernal size $= 3$, stride $= 2 \times 1$ and padding $= 1$. We use Adam optimizer with learning rate $= .001$, $\beta_1 = .9$ and $\beta_2 = .999$. We trained the network in 100 epochs with batch size $= 128$. Similar to the testing procedure in the Section 5.5.4, for a given testing trajectory, the network is applied on the segments of the samples, giving binary classification result for each segment. The final decision for the video is given by the majority vote of all the segment results of the testing trajectory.

Implementation Detail for LSTM and LSTM+attention

For LSTM [44], we input the entire 3D trajectory of the agent to the network instead of the 30-frame segment as in previous baselines. This allows the LSTM baseline to learn to recognize video-wise intentionality from an entire trajectory, rather than using the simple hand-crafted rules for aggregating segment-wise inference as described in Section 5.5.3. We use 10 dimensional hidden state and cell state, initialized with zero vectors at the beginning of each sequence. At the last frame, the hidden state is fed to a 10-by-2 fully connected network with softmax. The network is optimized using Stochastic Gradient Descent (SGD) with learning rate $= .001$ and momentum $= .9$ to minimize the cross-entropy loss.

For LSTM+attention, we used the attention mechanism proposed in [10], which models temporal attention as a bi-directional LSTM with 10-dimensional hidden and cell states. We use the same LSTM model described above to model the trajectory dynamics, jointly optimized with attention module using cross-entropy loss. The network is also optimized using SGD with learning rate $= .001$ and momentum $= .9$.

Implementation Detail for video based classification

We also provide three additional baselines, LSTM+ResNet, LSTM+ResNet+attention and R(2+1)D [99] with images sequences as input rather than 3D trajectories of agents. These baselines provide insight on the effectiveness of 3D trajectory as input feature. The image sequence is extracted at every 10 frames to reduce the total length. For each frame in this sequence, the RGB image within the bounding box of an agent is extracted, then resized to 224×224. For both LSTM+ResNet and LSTM+ResNet+attention baselines, a 512 dimensional feature is extracted after the average pooling layer, which will be used as input feature to the LSTM module. The hidden and cell states of the LSTM used in this experiment are both 512-d to accommodate the increase in dimensionality of the input features. An 512-by-2 fully-connected network is used to recognize the action of given agent is intentional or not. Both ResNet18 and LSTM (with attention module) are jointly trained using SGD with learning rate $= .001$ and momentum $= .9$. R(2+1)D is trained using Adam optimizer with learning rate $= .001$, $\beta_1 = .9$ and $\beta_2 = .999$.

Table 5.1: Quantitative result comparison between the ours and baseline algorithms, measured by mean classification accuracy and standard error of the mean (in parenthesis). 3D COM: 3D trajectory of the agent's center of mass

Methods	input	maya	mocap	youtube
LDA	3D COM	0.533 (0.060)	0.755 (0.014)	0.653 (0.017)
NN	3D COM	0.683 (0.052)	0.805 (0.023)	0.654 (0.014)
KSDA	3D COM	0.633 (0.048)	0.795 (0.022)	0.577 (0.013)
ResNet	3D COM	0.783 (0.058)	0.760 (0.025)	0.580 (0.019)
LSTM	3D COM	0.581 (0.232)	0.835 (0.082)	0.615 (0.057)
LSTM+attention	3D COM	0.504 (0.209)	0.671 (0.155)	0.505 (0.059)
LSTM+ResNet	RGB video	0.550 (0.200)	-	0.770 (0.036)
LSTM+ResNet+attention	RGB video	0.517 (0.089)	-	0.704 (0.079)
R(2+1)D	RGB video	0.500 (0.091)	-	0.609 (0.017)
Ours	3D	**0.950**	**0.827**	**0.785**

Quantitative Result

Table 5.1 shows the mean classification accuracy and its standard error for the four baseline methods in maya, mocap and youtube datasets. We use leave-one-pair-out cross-validation for the baseline experiments in maya dataset, and 10-fold cross-validation for mocap and youtube dataset. We did not calculate the mean accuracy for our method since our method does not need training thus the entire dataset is used as testing set without cross-validation. As shown in the table, the accuracy of our proposed algorithm is significantly higher than the accuracy of the baseline methods in intent-maya dataset. In intent-mocap and intent-youtube dataset our algorithm produces comparable results to the most accurate baseline methods. It is worth noting that our algorithm achieves these result without any supervision or training, comparing to all the baselines which are learning based methods.

As demonstrated by the above experiments, the algorithm described in this paper is general and can be applied to any video of an action. To prove this further, we decided to apply our approach to a new dataset that appeared long after we had submitted the first version of this paper.[6] Thus, this serves as an independent test on a data we had no access to during the design of our algorithm. The database in question is the Oops! database [29], which shows a number of unintentional actions collected from YouTube. We thus used our derived algorithm to identify these unintentional actions in the dataset. In this challenging task, our algorithms achieved 66.51% accuracy.

One may wonder why our result is significantly better than all the 3D baselines in the youtube dataset but only comparable to the best baseline in the mocap dataset, since they are both essentially the same type of data (3D human pose sequence). One possible explanation is related to the highly noisy samples. In intent-youtube dataset, the 3D trajectory of an agent is estimated from the 2D video rather than directly measured by sensors as in mocap dataset. This estimation process introduces significantly higher noise to the youtube dataset due to the limitation of the off-the-shelf 3D human pose estimation algorithm. When a powerful non-linear data-driven learning algorithm (like ResNet, KSDA and LSTM) is used to learn the underlying pattern in this dataset, it is more likely that the algorithm will overfit to the noise, ending up with higher testing error [33]. Our algorithm, on the other hand, directly examines the kinematics feature without training, thus avoiding this possible issue.

Table 5.2 also shows disadvantages of supervised methods in a biased dataset, which is almost always the case. This is particularly clear when examine the result of LSTM (3D) and LSTM+attention (3D) in intent-maya dataset using 10-fold cross-validation where the classification accuracy is even below the chance level of 50%. The reason for the low performance on the maya dataset is its careful design. The samples in the maya dataset are

---

[6]This experiment was added during the revision phase of this paper.

Table 5.2: Comparing leave-one-pair-out (LOPO) cross-validation versus 10-fold cross-validation on intent-maya dataset using LSTM and LSTM+attention.

cross-validation	LOPO	10-fold
LSTM (3D)	0.581 (0.232)	0.482 (0.103)
LSTM+attention (3D)	0.504 (0.209)	0.365 (0.142)

designed in intentional-nonintentional pairs. Within a pair, the background, objects, and illumination agents are all identical. The only difference is the kinematics of the agent, which is also designed to be as similar as possible while preserving the significant difference in the perception of intentionality. When we randomly partition the dataset for 10-fold cross-validation, some intentional (non-intentional) samples in the validation set might have a their non-intentional (intentional) counterpart in the training set. Due to the data-driven nature of the supervised models, the similarity between the training and testing samples tends to bias the network towards the wrong decision. This is particularly true for the models like LSTM and LSTM+attention, which are given a higher flexibility to learn not only the features, but also the rules for video-wise recognition of intent. Our algorithm, on the other hand, does not have this disadvantage due to its common knowledge based inference.

5.5.5 Qualitative Result

The result in last section shows that our algorithm achieves higher or comparable classification accuracy on the video-level to the baseline methods. However, it is unknown if our algorithm can return reasonable segment-level classification. Imagine an agent trips while walking, with walking occupying a significant portion of the video. An algorithm can give correct annotation (non-intentional) of the sequence even if the walking is labeled as non-intentional and tripping as intentional. To examine this possible issue, we provide qualitative result of segment/frame-level intent recognition by our algorithm on the three datasets (see Figure 5.5 for intent-maya dataset, Figure 5.6 for intentional actions and Figure 5.7 for non-intentional actions in intent-mocap dataset, see Figure 5.8 for intent-youtube dataset). These results shows that our algorithm can correctly recognizing intent of the agent on both video level and segment level. For example, in the "Tripping" sequence, our algorithm correctly annotates that the action (walking) is intentional before the 70th frame and unintentional thereafter, accurately reflecting the moment that the agent trips.

5.5.6 Effect of keypoints occlusion

Since our algorithm depends on the estimation of the agent's center of mass, it is necessary to study the robustness of our algorithm against keypoints occlusion in the pose estimation.

We design three experiments to simulate a variety of cases of occlusions on skeleton keypoints: 1. A random joint is always occluded across all samples, similar to the cases where one of the sensors (or mocap markers) is defective; 2. A random joint is occluded per agent, which simulate the cases where a keypoint is occluded consistently for an agent; 3. A random joint is occluded per frame, which is to simulate a highly noisy center of mass estimate. Typically, the occlusion on a specific keypoint occurs consecutively across several frames, during which estimation of agent's center of mass is biased. For our algorithm, a biased but smooth estimate of the center of mass is less problematic than a highly noisy estimate, which might produce an artificial increase of mechanical energy (due to the jittering

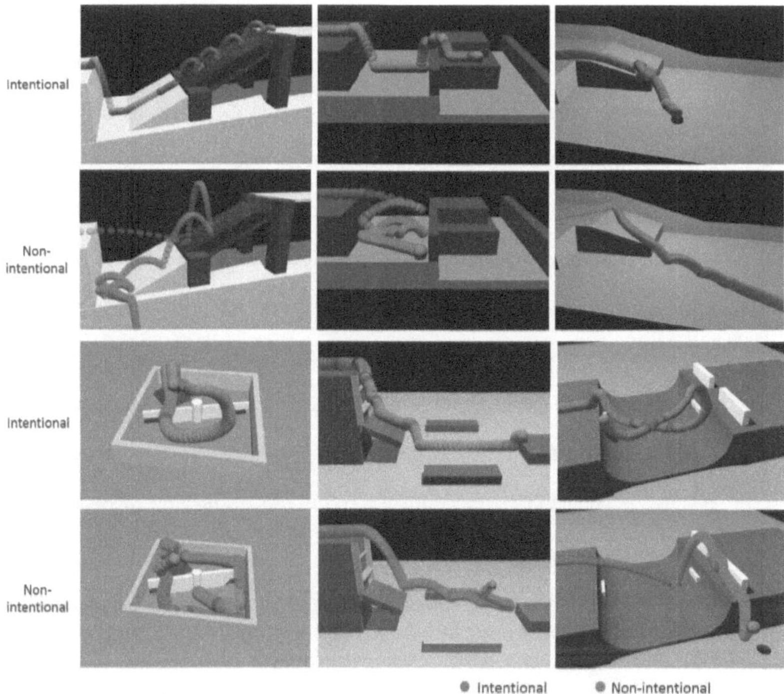

Figure 5.5: Qualitative result of our algorithm testing on intent-maya dataset. The full model with all concepts is used. Blue (red) indicates that our algorithm recognizes the movement of the agent as intentional (non-intentional) at that specific time. The ground truth annotation is shown on the left of the figure.

movement). Thus, we occlude random joints per frame to simulate this highly noisy estimation of the center of mass, which tests our algorithm in a highly unfavorable setup. The keypoint occlusion experiment is only conducted on the intent-mocap and intent-youtube dataset, since the intent-maya dataset does not have keypoints defined for its ball agent.

Table 5.3 shows the result of our algorithm on intent-mocap and intent-youtube dataset with the three types of keypoint occlusion mentioned above. To provide a measurement of uncertainty, we repeat the three experiments with randomly selected keypoints for occlusion and report the mean accuracy and its standard error. As we can see, when only one joint is consistently occluded, either across all samples or per agent, there is no significant negative impact on our algorithm. In the worse case occlusion we designed for our algorithm, there is a drop in the classification accuracy due to the inaccurate estimation on the change of total mechanical energy induced by the noisy estimation of the center of mass, which is consistent with what we described earlier. Notice that we did not perform preprocessing to smooth the trajectory of the center of mass or infer the missing joint, which can be done to improve the performance.

Table 5.3: Quantitative result on our algorithm with occluded keypoints, measured by mean classification accuracy and standard error of the mean (in parenthesis).

Occlusion	intent-mocap	intent-youtube
None	0.827	0.785
1 joint all sample	0.833 (0.008)	0.769 (0.011)
1 joint per agent	0.808 (0.006)	0.767 (0.003)
1 joint per frame	0.712 (0.021)	0.624 (0.006)

5.5.7 Ablation study

The result in the previous section shows that our algorithm is effective on recognizing intentionality from the trajectory of the agents. However, it is still unknown that if all the common sense concepts we introduced in the Section 5.3 are necessary. We conduct an ablation study on the proposed algorithm to study this problem. In this experiment, we started with a model including only Concept 1, and gradually adding each common concept until reaching the full model with all four concepts. When classify with the ablated model, we directly apply the method described in Section 5.5.3 to I_* - the output of the model with ablated Concepts. For example, when only C1 is used, $I_* = I_{C1}$, with I_{C1} defined in equation (5.1). For the ablated model with C1+2+4, we calculate the output of the model using Algorithm 2 but with I_{C2} as input instead of I_{C3}.

Table 5.4: Quantitative result of our algorithm with ablation, measured by mean classification accuracy and standard error of the mean (in parenthesis)

dataset	1	1+2	1+2+3	1+2+4	1+2+3+4
maya	0.500	0.667	0.667	0.783	0.950
mocap	0.500	0.571	0.534	0.737	0.827
youtube	0.500	0.519	0.501	0.735	0.785

5.5.8 Analysis on the ablation result

The result of the ablation study is shown in Table 5.4. When the C1 is the only concept used in the model, the classification accuracy is no greater than random chance for both maya and mocap datasets. With more common sense concepts included, the classification accuracy increases, indicating that the proposed common sense concepts are all necessary to achieve an accurate recognition. One may notice that the accuracy of C1+2+3 is no higher than C1+2 and may argue that C3 is not necessary for this reason. However, this argument is challenged by the result of C1+2+4 is less accurate result than C1+2+3+4, indicating that C3 is necessary in when combined with C4 (rather than C2) to further improve the accuracy. As mentioned in Section 5.3.2, the four concepts combined to form a common knowledge system for intent recognition.

5.6   Discussion and conclusion

The result in the previous section shows that our algorithm can achieve significantly superior or comparable accuracy to a range of learning based method on three datasets. The result also shows the necessity of each of the common knowledge concepts in the proposed algorithm. By modeling those concepts that defines intentionality, our algorithm does not need labeled data, nor it is a learning-based algorithm, thus shy away from the potential sampling bias in training set. Since the algorithm does not need training and composes only rules that derived from human common sense, the method is less computationally demanding and more interpretable than most of the deep learning based algorithms. The performance on the three datasets also shows the general applicability of the proposed common concept algorithm on different types of agents.

The result also shows that the classification accuracy of our algorithm is decreasing from maya to mocap to youtube dataset. One possible explanation is the lack of accuracy in the estimated center of mass of the agent in the mocap and youtube datasets. Intent-maya dataset only contains sphere-like agents, whose trajectory of the center of mass is readily available with high precision. However, in the mocap and youtube datasets, the center of mass has to be estimated from the skeleton of the agent, which is more accurate

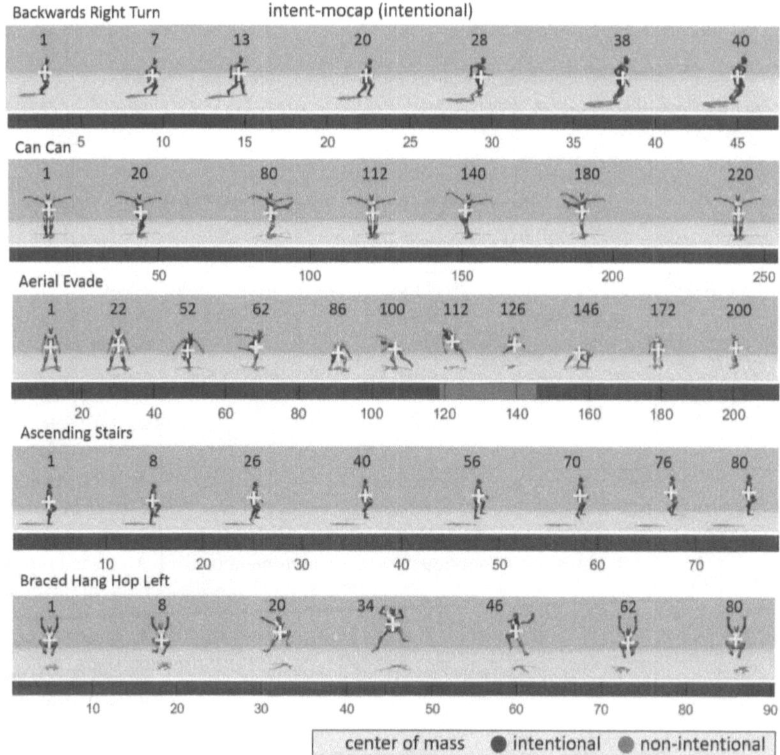

Figure 5.6: Qualitative result of our algorithm testing on intent-mocap datasets. All samples shown here contains intentional actions. The full model with all concepts is used. The colorbar indicates the intentionality judgement by our algorithm at each frame, blue for intentional and red for non-intentional. The number above the agent is the corresponding frame index in the sequence. The action name is shown on the top-left corner of each sequence which corresponds to the animation name in mixamo dataset. We applied median filter on I_{C4} with windows size 30 to increase smoothness or the result.

in mocap dataset than in youtube dataset (but both worse than the maya dataset), potentially explaining the drop of classification accuracy in the yotube dataset comparing to the
mocap dataset. One should also notice that the proposed algorithm does not claim nor
implement any novelty in 3D human pose estimation, which by itself is a challenging and
open problem.

Table 5.5: Cases for intentionality of the interaction between A and B.

Case	A action	B action	A $\rightarrow$ B interaction	Example
1	intentional	intentional	intentional	A punched B in a boxing game.
2	intentional	intentional	non-intentional	A is walking backward but B is walking normally. A bumped into B without noticing B.
3	non-intentional	intentional	non-intentional	A is on a bike out of control and crashed into B.
4	non-intentional	non-intentional	non-intentional	A crashed into B when both of them are ice-skiing and cannot control their movement.
5	intentional	non-intentional	intentional	A catches B while B tripped over an obstacle.

Another significant future direction of the study is to infer intentionality when the action
involves multiple agents. When social interactions are involved, the inference of intentionality can become much more complex. Table 5.5 provides a rudimentary anecdotal analysis
on the potential cases of intentionality in a two-agent system without considering the environmental context. As shown in the table, the relationship is complex, but not lacking
of rules. For example, If the action conducted by agent A is non-intentional, it is likely

that the interaction from agent A to agent B is also non-intentional. However, the *reverse equality* may not hold. Thus, we argue that to consider solving this complicated multi-agent problem, it is necessary to address the that of a single agent first, which is what we did in the present work.

In conclusion, we proposed a common knowledge based unsupervised computer vision system for recognizing intent of an agent, specifically whether the action of the agent is intentional or not. The problem is significant due to the essential role played by the intent recognition in human's social life. Any machine that intended to work and live with human might benefit from intent recognition to achieve a smooth human-machine interaction. Recognition of intentionality (intentional vs unintentional) is a first step towards this goal. Our algorithm, to our knowledge, provides the first common knowledge based computer vision algorithm for the recognition of intentionality. Comparing to the modern computer vision and pattern recognition systems, whose majority are data-driven learning methods that require a large amount of training data, our system achieves this high-level vision task without the need for training data, but achieves higher or comparable result on multiple datasets to the baselines. The effectiveness of our algorithm not only provides a potential way to address the problem of automatic visual recognition of intent, but also performing high-level reasoning without using training data by leveraging human commonsense concepts.

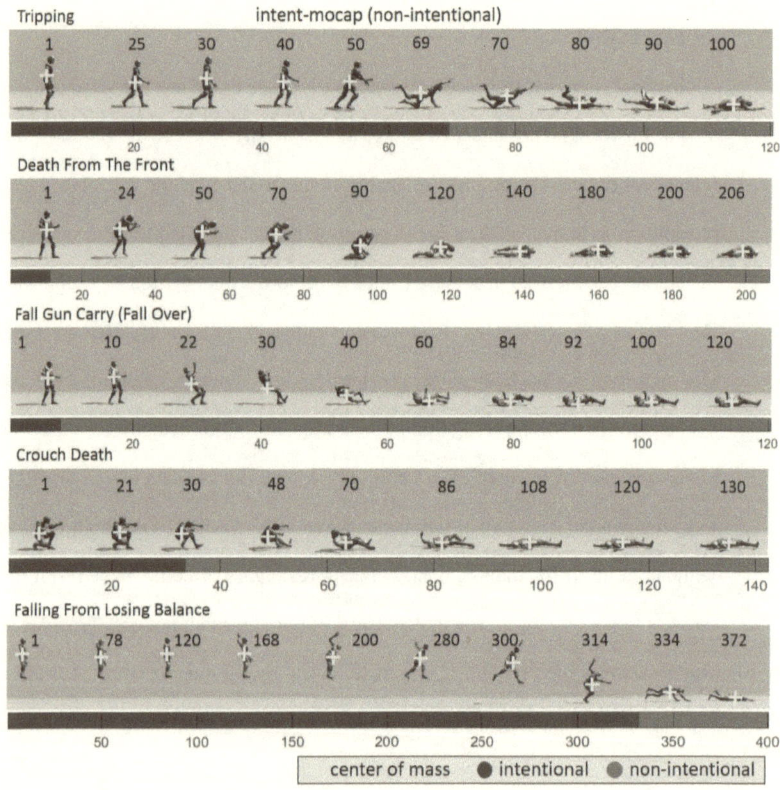

Figure 5.7: Qualitative result of our algorithm testing on intent-mocap datasets. All samples shown here contains non-intentional actions. The full model with all concepts is used. The same method used in Figure 5.6 is applied to generated this images.

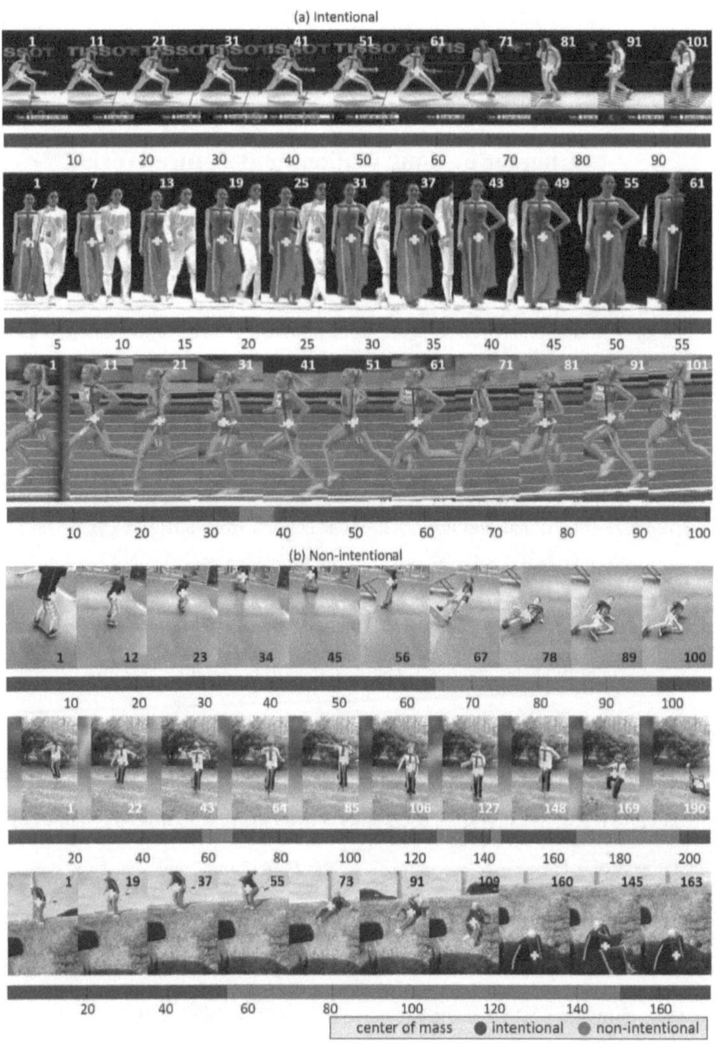

Figure 5.8: Qualitative result of our algorithm testing on intent-youtube datasets. Each sequence contains 10 samples uniformed sampled across time. The colorbar depicts intentionality judgement by our algorithm at each frame. Median filter with windows size 30 frames is also applied for visual presentation.

Chapter 6: Contributions and Future Work

This dissertation presents a series of studies focusing on modeling intentional and non-intentional actions in human brain and machines. The fMRI study first shows that the human brain employs a number of regions to perform intentionality recognition. Inspired by the brain's mirroring mechanism, two GAN-based algorithms are designed to generate and recognize intentional and non-intentional actions from abstract geometric animation and realistic in-the-wild videos respectively. Inspired by the human perception on self-propelled motion, a common knowledge based algorithm is proposed for intentionality recognition on both abstract and realistic agents with no need for training.

In the introduction, we discussed the three-level understanding of complex system. From a research perspective, the Computational/Algorithmic understanding and Implementational brain research can inspire each other. Given the results from the studies in Chapter 3, Chapter 4 and Chapter 5, we can revisit the fMRI study and see if we can formulate more specific hypothesis on the brain implementation of intentionality recognition. The following discussion will solely focusing on classifying action intentionality from abstract geometric animation, which is the exclusive focus of the fMRI study.

If the computational model proposed in Chapter 5 can be viewed as a hypothetical simplified model for intentionality recognition in brain, then it is possible for us to speculate the necessary component in the brain to implement such computation. Concept 1 and 2 indicate the necessity of a self-propelled motion and an external-force movement detector in the brain. The Concept 3 indicates a necessary causal inference between the EFM and SPM. Concept 4 proposes a default preservation mechanism of intentionality. [32] has studies brain regions for "physical engine" with a task of mental simulation of a falling lego-like structure. However, this experiment shows potential brain regions for simulation, rather than recognition. For biological motion, it is known that there exist mirror neuron systems in the brain that combines the generation and perception, however this is not known yet for the physical movement. From the study in Chapter 2, we know that the area responsible for the classification are most likely located in Biological motion, Body, ToM and MT. Thus a further study can be designed to probe the neural substrate supporting the detection of EFM. This can be achieved by designing stimulus contrast of intentional movement contains both SPM and EFM and intentional movement with only SPM.

For the future work regarding the recognition of action intentionality on a single abstract geometric agent, there is still a main question on how do we generalize intentionality recognition from human body to abstract geometric objects as shown at the very beginning of this dissertation in Figure 1.1. Do we first learn human intentional kinematics, then abstract the kinematics to apply to the abstract agent? Or do we directly learn intentional kinematics from our early childhood playing with toys (most of them composes abstract geometric objects)? If we construct a machine learning algorithm that learn from human intentional behavior, it is possible for it to generalize to abstract objects?

Another direction of future work is non-kinematic based intentionality recognition. This disseration solely focusing on the kinematic features for recognition of intentionality, from abstract agents to human agents. However, same agent's kinematics might leads to totally different intentionality perception depending on the context when the action happened. For example, a human agent kick a football to a gate would be generally intentional, but if the ball hit a passenger instead it is generally perceived as non-intentional. Although the action kinematics "kick" is the same, the consequence and context of the action is different, thus making the intentionality perception differ.

This work can also be generalized to other fields with more abstract human actions. For example, a data breach, can be intentional or unintentional. Similarly, one can also decide other electronic or mechanical malfunction is due to an accidental failure, or intentional sabotage. When the proposed method is used in these applications, one should pay particular attention to the difference in the underlying problems. The study presented here, focuses on the *human perception* of intentionality. This focus dictates the algorithmic design and validation method. These more generic applications on the other hand, focuses on unveiling the ground-truth intentionality behind a pattern, which is generally a much more difficult job. When lacking context, the human perception of intentoinality can still operate, potentially assigning a different intentionality then the ground-truth, which is acceptable in this study but might not be the case in other generic applications.

A car doesn't have legs like a horse. A plane doesn't have a pair of flappy wings like a bird, a machine doesn't have to behave like its biological counterpart even if it has to interact with one. The necessity of intent recognition in machines can be drastically decreased when the intentionality of human mental state hidden from the naked eye once become accessible to machines. This could be achieved with a direct and comprehensive brain-machine interface with intentionality encoding / decoding capability. At that moment, the machine will serve as a bridge to mutual understanding between humans as it "opens" human mind. But will it be beneficial to the society? Or it will actually brought down the productivity? For the human are attuned to intention recognition from millions of years of evolution, it might not be good to share our mind even if everybody were willing to do so. These ethical questions should also be discussed and studied in the future.

During the work of this dissertation, studies starts to emerge on this topic of intentionality recognition in the field of computer vision and machine intelligence [29]. It is my hope that this specific field can continue to grow and mature for its scientific value and potential on improving human life. And it is also my hope that this series of works can serve as a tiny building block on much better algorithms, a much deeper understanding of our human brain, and a much better future for the human race.